BETTER, NOT BITTER

BETTER, NOT BITTER

LIVING ON PURPOSE
IN THE PURSUIT
OF RACIAL JUSTICE

YUSEF SALAAM

GRAND CENTRAL
PUBLISHING

New York   Boston

Grand Central Publishing
Hachette Book Group
1290 Avenue of the Americas, New York, NY 10104
grandcentralpublishing.com
twitter.com/grandcentralpub

First Edition: May 2021

Grand Central Publishing is a division of Hachette Book Group, Inc. The Grand Central Publishing name and logo is a trademark of Hachette Book Group, Inc.

The publisher is not responsible for websites (or their content) that are not owned by the publisher.

The Hachette Speakers Bureau provides a wide range of authors for speaking events. To find out more, go to www.hachettespeakersbureau.com or call (866) 376-6591.

Scripture quotations marked (NIV) are taken from the Holy Bible, New International Version®, NIV®. Copyright © 1973, 1978, 1984, 2011 by Biblica, Inc.™ Used by permission of Zondervan. All rights reserved worldwide. www.zondervan.com. The "NIV" and "New International Version" are trademarks registered in the United States Patent and Trademark Office by Biblica, Inc.™

Unless otherwise noted, all quotations from the Qur'an are taken from the Saheeh International translation. Copyright © 1997 by Abul-Qasim Publishing House.
Quotation from Qur'an 28:61 from the Marmaduke Pickthall translation of the Qur'an, republished by the Folio Society, 2012.
Unless otherwise noted, all photos are courtesy of the author.

Library of Congress Cataloging-in-Publication Data
Names: Salaam, Yusef, 1974– author.
Title: Better, not bitter : living on purpose in the pursuit of racial justice / Yusef Salaam.
Description: First edition. | New York : Grand Central Publishing, 2021. | Summary: "They didn't know who they had." So begins Yusef Salaam telling his story. No one's life is the sum of the worst things that happened to them, and during Yusef Salaam's seven years of wrongful incarceration as one of the Central Park Five, he grew from child to man, and gained a spiritual perspective on life. Yusef learned that we're all "born on purpose, with a purpose." Despite having confronted the racist heart of America while being "run over by the spiked wheels of injustice," Yusef channeled his energy and pain into something positive, not just for himself but for other marginalized people and communities. Better, Not Bitter is the first time that one of the now Exonerated Five is telling his individual story, in his own words. Yusef writes his narrative: growing up Black in central Harlem in the '80s, being raised by a strong, fierce mother and grandmother, his years of incarceration, his reentry, and exoneration. Yusef connects these stories to lessons and principles he learned that gave him the power to survive through the worst of life's experiences. He inspires readers to accept their own path, to understand their own sense of purpose. With his intimate personal insights, Yusef unpacks the systems built and designed for profit and the oppression of Black and Brown people. He inspires readers to channel their fury into action, and through the spiritual, to turn that anger and trauma into a constructive force that lives alongside accountability and mobilizes change. This memoir is an inspiring story that grew out of one of the gravest miscarriages of justice, one that not only speaks to a moment in time or the rage-filled present, but reflects a 400-year history of a nation's inability to be held accountable for its sins. Yusef Salaam's message is vital for our times, a motivating resource for enacting change. Better, Not Bitter has the power to soothe, inspire, and transform. It is a galvanizing call to action.— Provided by publisher.
Identifiers: LCCN 2020054033 | ISBN 9781538705001 (hardcover) | ISBN 9781538704981 (ebook)
Subjects: LCSH: Salaam, Yusef, 1974– | Prisoners—New York (State)—New York—Biography. | False imprisonment—New York (State)—New York | Judicial error—New York (State)—New York. | Discrimination in criminal justice administration—New York (State)—New York.
Classification: LCC HV9468.S244 A3 2021 | DDC 365/.6092 [B]—dc23
LC record available at https://lccn.loc.gov/2020054033

ISBNs: 978-1-5387-0500-1 (hardcover), 978-1-5387-0498-1 (ebook)

Printed in the United States of America

LSC-C

Printing 1, 2021

For my mother, Sharonne Salaam;
my sister, Ace; and my brother, Shaf

Contents

BETTER, NOT BITTER

Born on Purpose, with a Purpose

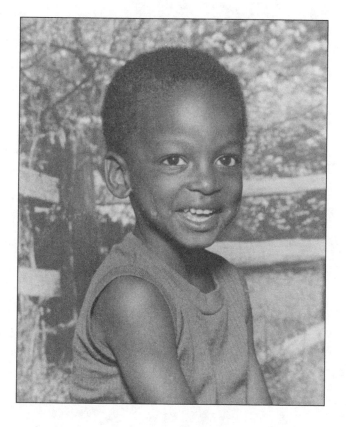

THEY DIDN'T KNOW WHO THEY HAD.

I say this often, and most people think it is something I figured out *after* being imprisoned for a crime I did not commit. It is not. From very early on, I innately knew that I had a destiny that existed beyond the one the criminal justice system attempted to assign to me. I just needed to live long enough for that purpose to come to fruition.

And to be honest, my survival wasn't the only thing at stake. My physical survival, yes, but also my mental and emotional endurance.

They didn't know who they had.

In 1989, I was run over by the spiked wheels of justice. I was vilified in such a way that I became a pariah, a scourge. Within the first few weeks of the accusations that would turn Antron McCray, Kevin Richardson, Raymond Santana, Korey Wise, and myself—then known as the Central Park Five—into poster children for Black deviance, a tsunami of media rolled out the proverbial red carpet, leading us to our destruction at the hands of the American justice system.

On the day I was convicted, my hope died. It would take

years before it was resurrected again. I was sixteen years old when I stood in the hallway of the courthouse and someone ran up to me saying, "They have a verdict!" In that moment, I truly believed that we'd be exonerated. Surely they would see that we didn't do this, I thought. I'd been out on bail up until that point, so although I'd had to endure the questions, the intense media scrutiny, I was still giving my mom a kiss before bed at night. I was still talking to my cousins, talking to my friends.

Guilty.

That verdict shattered me. I was a child. But I didn't get to go home with my mom and turn myself in later. They put the handcuffs on me right there and then. No hugs. No long good-byes. No letting me change my clothes or shoes. They took us away immediately. I felt a profound sense of powerlessness in that moment, a moment I wouldn't wish on my worst enemy. My body shook with fear. I'm still not sure how I found the strength to stand up. *What, do you mean right now?* I felt like I was being led to the slaughterhouse. Aside from child molestation, rape was the worst crime to go to jail for. They were supposed to send us back to the juvenile detention center, but they didn't. Instead, they intentionally sent us directly to Rikers Island, a notoriously violent prison from which many men never returned.

I'm gonna die.

They tried to kill me.

They stole years from us. From me.

But I didn't die.

Because I was somehow always clear that I was born on

purpose, with a purpose. With that knowledge, I was able to keep my mind free, even when my body was imprisoned.

When I think about how I was able to survive this thing and why I believe in the power of purpose in a person's life, I think about the ancient stories of Abraham (ع)[1] found in both the Bible and the Qur'an. Stories I uncovered only after deep-diving into these sacred texts while in prison.

Abraham (ع) was chosen. He was called to a specific assignment. When they threw him into the fire, all he had to say was "God, help me!" and God told the fire to be cool and safe. That's what this journey has been like for me. Of course, I'm not Abraham (ع). I'm no prophet. But I do believe I have a purpose that made it so that despite the things designed to kill me—the racism, the criminal system of injustice, the attempted assault while in prison—it was God who told the prison to be cool and safe for me. So I didn't suffer the same fate of others accused of and imprisoned for rape. The code didn't apply to me for some reason. There was, I believe, a light that the guards and other prisoners saw in and around me. A light that made them say, "You don't belong here." That doesn't mean it was easy, not by any means. I had hard and difficult days. But I felt this sense of having a veil, a hedge of protection, following and covering me everywhere I went.

My story is not your typical "how I've overcome" narrative.

---

[1] Please note: I have used (ع) throughout the text as a sign of reverence. Muslims are not allowed to mention the name of any prophet without saying عليه اسالم, which means "Peace be upon him."

I've been so grateful for the ways in which the story of the now Exonerated Five has been told via documentaries and the recent Netflix limited series. Ava DuVernay's *When They See Us* and all the subsequent interviews may have given you a taste of what some of my life was like after that fateful day in April 1989, but my life did not begin or end that day; my life is more than the sum of the worst things that happened to me. Now is the time for me to tell my *whole* story.

I not only hope to share who I was then and who I am now, but also what I want to tell you about most is who I was before 1989. I want to tell you about the foundation laid by both my family and my faith, which ensured that I would not only survive this awful injustice but also thrive in the midst of it.

I also want you to know that no matter where you come from or what circumstances you may find yourself in, you *can* thrive in the midst of your trials.

I have a somewhat mystical perspective when it comes to my experience. I firmly believe that when you look at what transpired in my life—between then and now—what you see is the hand of God. You may ask, how is that possible? How can a terrible injustice such as the one I lived with for almost twenty-five years be representative of anything divine at work?

I believe that everything that's happening *to* you is actually happening *for* you. Everything we experience in life—from our greatest joys to our deepest pain and hardship—is shaping and creating us. It's preparing us for what we will need later on in our lives. I was ripped out of society and lodged back in the womb of America, what some in America would call "the belly of the beast." Like many Black men and women, I was in a place where I was forced to be dependent on the system that in its creation is designed to use and harm Black bodies for profit. And it's a dependence that can become too familiar, that you can feel too accustomed to, if you're not careful. Far too often men and women are physically released back into society who aren't mentally, emotionally, or spiritually ready. They experience that rebirth too soon. They aren't taught how to detach from the incubator, so to speak. They are still dependent on being fed by a deeply dysfunctional system. But when the cell doors shut, I knew—even at such an early age—that if I was not careful to protect my mind and heart, I could become attached to the process of getting my nourishment from a system that didn't care about me at all. I had to keep reminding myself that this experience was one that God would use to teach me something I would need in the future. I now firmly believe that I was being stretched, broken, and adjusted in a different way in order to be birthed back into society as a person who now is fearless.

One clear and present example of God's hand in all this is the fact that the very person who castigated us, the person who—without knowing us—hated us the most and spent $85,000 for ads in national newspapers to bring back the death penalty in order to poison public opinion against us, would ultimately become the forty-fifth president of the United States. God knew I needed to have a backbone that would allow me to not cower in the face of it all. I needed to have a level of strength that would allow me to continue to stand tall in the face of my vilifier and continue to speak truth to power.

I think every person who has been to jail instinctively responds to the sound of cell doors closing. The steel clanging of bars and the echo that lasts long after the door has shut. That sound is a trigger for me that I still can't shake, sending shivers and chills through my body. A few years ago I went to Sing Sing to do my TED Talk. I was excited to be able to share my story with men who might have been struggling in the same ways I once had. At first, I tried to bring my laptop, phone, and tablet inside, and the guard was like, "This is jail. Don't you remember? You can't bring any of that in here." But I had forgotten.

Ultimately, I left everything I'd prepared on my laptop and phone outside the prison and entered with just a few written notes and my mind. But when I heard those cell doors close, the clanging and the echo, it pulled me back to my fifteen- and sixteen- and twenty-one-year-old selves. For a moment, I panicked. My blood ran cold and that familiar sinking feeling lodged itself in my gut. *They know I'm just a visitor, right? They are not going to leave me in here, right?* The trauma of my past was entwined in me; it had connected itself to my body.

My experience taught me how to deal with fear. Like many have said, fear is nothing more than false evidence appearing as reality, and I believe that to be true. After all, it was fear of Black and Brown bodies that led America to damn the five of us, for the false evidence linking us to a crime to be taken for fact. When you conquer a fear once, you will find yourself being more courageous the next time you are faced with it. Sometimes fear is allowed to be present for a while; sometimes we should permit ourselves to experience fear in order to grow from it. In doing so, we grow more courageous and we can share those lessons fear taught us as we move toward operating in our purpose. You see, everybody was born on purpose. Even the thief and the murderer. I've learned through my own life that, as much as we despise it and wish it weren't true, there's a necessity for evil, for difficulties. There is no light without darkness.

You and I were born on purpose and for a purpose. This idea becomes crystal clear when we realize that when our parents created us, the person we would ultimately become was one of over four hundred million options. We have sperm racing toward an egg, and the odds of us being us are astronomical. Think about it! There was intention there. Part of understanding my story is reconciling the concept that we all have a great thing to do in this world once we realize who we are.

Haven't we all, at some point in time, wondered, *What am I here for? What am I supposed to be doing?* And especially if, like me, you find yourself in a less than favorable circumstance, these questions are often first and foremost in your mind. But the thing is, I've found that the answers to those questions lie in what is showing up in my life. The key is to be still long enough to really listen to what your experiences and circumstances are telling you. Once we do that, we just might find ourselves saying, "Oh, I was *supposed* to go through this," or "I was meant to grow through that." I hope those two perspectives will change your outlook and your movements in life, as they did mine.

Instead of deciding to believe that their terrible circumstance actually has the hand of God written on it, many people will question God. Some even go as far as cursing God. They want to know, "Why is this happening to me?" And to a certain extent, I understand why we are prone to do this. The Exonerated Five were children. We were fourteen, fifteen, and sixteen years old. Why would such a traumatic event be allowed to happen to five innocent kids? A few of my brothers in this experience felt this way. But, personally, I would never have been able to survive if I didn't allow the experience to deepen my faith. My time in prison became a spiritual awakening that I'm grateful to be able to finally share. It was part of my metamorphosis. And just like the caterpillar that must wrap itself in a chrysalis and endure a season of waiting until its full beauty is realized, I, too, had to be wrapped up for a season in order to be revealed to the world as the person I am today.

As my mother always says, "Nobody leaves here alive." The wealthiest place on earth has never been Africa, where there is gold and diamonds; or the Middle East, where there's oil. The richest place on earth is the graveyard. It's the place where everyone's unfulfilled hopes, dreams, and aspirations have been laid to rest. My challenge to you is this: No matter what life has taken you through, try to live full and die empty.

So it's important that you don't just read stories like mine and then go about your life, business as usual. Take a look at the evil that showed up in my life and figure out what your light will be. What will be your purpose in this moment? Whether you're a child of a former enslaved African or a child of a former slave owner, how do you use your present-day privilege to help the cause of racial injustice? Can I leverage the resources I have and start donating to causes and organizations that help people who have been marginalized and trampled upon? Can I give my time and skills to work with communities and organizations at the grassroots level? Can I take my voice and use it to defend the voiceless, to have the difficult conversations needed to change hearts and minds? These are the questions I hope you ask, even as you unpack what your own purpose is.

Introduction

In the wake of George Floyd's last words, "I can't breathe"; the ambush of Breonna Taylor by police in Louisville, Kentucky; and all the protests that followed, there have been many stories written about injustice and systemic racism. In most cases, however, these articles capture only one part of the story: the impact of an event or the collective action that followed. Often, we tend to lean on binaries that help move our agendas along, both in general and in the realm of social justice. We hear about either the looters or the peaceful protesters. Never about the oppressive forces that led to such an outpouring of rage and grief being expressed in the streets. Never about the work and progress accomplished as a result of the resistance. In order to mobilize for change, we must be able to connect the dots between a murder in Minneapolis and brutality in Biloxi; between redlining in Chicago and Black homelessness rates in Los Angeles. And there's another side to these headlines. A more intimate perspective that is just as impactful in changing minds and hearts is the story of Breonna Taylor moving from Michigan to Kentucky for a better life. It's a story of George Floyd serving at-risk youth with a Bible study group in Houston. Knowing the collective narrative is important. Knowing the story of the individual is transformative.

Linking the individual narrative with the collective one paints a clearer picture of what's *actually* happening to Black and Brown people in this country. No room is left for speculation or assumption. That said, it's vital to continue telling the earthly, collective part of any story, of our story. How white supremacy embedded in the American system of injustice infringed on the rights of five Black boys and their families. How Korey Wise experienced deep, terrible trauma while behind bars. How Raymond Santana returned to prison because he was unable to find meaningful employment, making it more difficult for him to bounce back from our ordeal. Ours is the story of five boys who were brought low only to rise again because the truth can never stay buried. Ours is the story of five boys who were buried alive and forgotten. Ours is the story of a system that forgot that we were seeds. The story of how this system is actually alive and sick. How it is operating exactly as it was designed. How Black and Brown and poor people in marginalized communities are unable to financially fight against this system, and that's by design. How anybody who is trapped in that marginal space becomes part of the oil that keeps the machine moving. All of that grit and grime, the trials and triumphs, the injustice and inequity, four hundred years of American history, are part of a necessary conversation that I will continue to have as I write and speak around the world.

Yet, I do know there is more. So much more.

The Central Park jogger case is actually a love story between God and His people about a system of injustice placed on trial itself, then toppled, in order to produce what amounts to a miracle in modern time. But as the old saying goes: "When you're walking through hell, keep on walking." There is always something on the other side. There is purpose on the other side. Sure, it's hard to see it that way. You can't always see the path, even when you're on it. But one day, just like I did, you'll turn around and reflect on the journey and say, "My God, look at what I went through. This didn't happen to me, but this happened for me. I came out stronger." Will there be indelible scars? Yes, of course. The way I move through the world and how I see myself have forever been altered by the levels of pain and uncertainty I had to climb my way out of. But I returned to society and learned to live on my own two feet. And now I get to show people how they can live on theirs. In the immortal words of the great modern philosopher Cardi B, "Knock me down nine times, but I get up ten."

Islam says, "Don't ask for help from anyone or anything except for God. There is nothing worthy of worship except God." So while family, friends, and mentors are important, when it comes to who is driving my life, I'm thinking that God is over and above even the saints or my ancestors. God is the One who is the author and the controller of this whole thing. We really don't have control. Our control and happiness come from being in sync with God. Whatever happens—the good, the bad, or the ugly—our acceptance opens us up to receive peace, harmony, and comfort. We cannot force a square into a space that wants only a circle. We simply say, "Man, God is good." Let's release ourselves from the pressure of being in control.

I'll never forget what Les Brown said to me a few years back. He said, "Yusef, I tell people all the time, it's not a matter of whether you fall in life, because you will fall. When you fall, try to land on your back because if you can look up, you can get up."

We all have the power to come back. I chose to believe that if I surrendered my control, God would never leave me. That was what helped me come back better and not bitter.

To be clear, my story does not begin with the Central Park jogger case. It begins with a young Black boy growing up in Harlem with a fierce mother who is incredibly loving and extremely protective of her children. It begins with a village of support and love surrounding me and infusing in me a confidence that would serve me greatly later. And just as my story doesn't begin with the Central Park Five trial, it doesn't end with the exoneration nor the multimillion-dollar settlement from the City of New York. Threaded through it all is how I've taken the injustice of a system that tried to destroy me and turned it inside out into a life of service. What I've lived through so far has required that I accept even the ugly circumstances I've experienced as God's will for my life, in order to be equipped to embrace the future. Acceptance—more than even forgiveness—is what is necessary for our forward movement. And acceptance can absolutely live alongside our demand for accountability from those who have wronged us. That's ultimately what this book is about.

What happened to the now Exonerated Five was a tragedy on the ground level, in the earthly realm. We were criminalized and dehumanized. But parallel to that was another reality. A greater intention. Spiritually, I had to say, "Wow, look at God!" No one could have created a story as dynamic as this.

My hope is that when you read this book, this stance can be applied to your own life. Evaluate it and realize that everything is ultimately purposeful. You have a purpose. Consider Joseph (ع) from the Bible. Or Yusuf (ع) in the Qur'an. His trials were only a drop in the bucket when we consider his victories. Consider the stories of Harriet Tubman and Frederick Douglass and Fannie Lou Hamer. We have these narratives that guide us, and too often we write them off as simply stories to uplift us. But they are not just about one person living one life, but rather they are complex narratives with the potential to reveal something about our own existence. They show us that we, too, can have personal power. We can be triumphant. We don't have to fall in life and stay down. We can get up. We are all favored. And in a way, that's what I hope this book does for every person who reads it.

When I look at my life post-release and how people celebrate the fact that we endured this awful thing, I always say, "What happened to me and for me can happen to you and for you as well." You may look at people and put them on these pedestals, but really, we are all servants. The more enlightened we become, the more humble we become. So, more than anything, when you close this book, I want you to dream again. I want my story to give you hope. I want you to say to yourself, "I'm going to try to take advantage of every opportunity I'm given. All the visions I have, let me carve out time to do it."

Yusef Salaam

ONE

The Escape

We are at war / The bulk of which will not be physical /
The bulk of which is mental...

YUSEF SALAAM

From the days immediately after
I was released to one of my first
experiences with meaningful
employment. I felt respected, and
like I was making an important
step toward a successful life.

"WHAT DO YOU WANT TO EAT?"

It was gray outside. The clouds were dense, hovering just above our heads. My mother, my sister, my mother's friend Ayesha Grice, and her niece Beverly all stood outside the car waiting with huge smiles. They were picking me up from prison. Finally. Still wearing my prison jacket, I melted into their hugs. All I could think about was putting one foot in front of the other, making sure that the release was actually happening. It was both beautiful and frightening to be out.

The night before, I'd tossed and turned with anxiety. I didn't want to go to sleep. *What if I don't wake up? What if somebody kills me just before I leave?*

Leaving the adult facility didn't feel real. I was finally going home, but I was terrified. It felt like I was escaping. Like I was a fugitive, and at any moment they were going to say there had been a terrible mistake and return me to my cell. But I was free. I'm fairly sure that I didn't really celebrate until I was back home, sitting in my apartment, trying on my clothes. I stayed up for thirty-six hours after my release just trying to take it all in: seeing my family's faces, our home I hadn't seen in almost seven years, the noise of the city streets, now loud and unignorable even though it had once simply been an unnoticed daily sound track playing in the background of my life.

But once in the car, I had my first decision to make. A relatively simple one, I suppose, but to have the power to make any kind of decision felt monumental. I'm not sure anyone around me at the time really understood how abnormal it felt to actually have a *choice* in something, even something as seemingly mundane as what to eat for breakfast.

"Man, I don't know. I could eat anything," I responded.

Only miles down the road from Clinton Correctional Facility in Dannemora, New York, we stopped at an IHOP. I sat down in the booth, still pondering this surreal new world I had found myself in, feeling very overwhelmed with trying to process it all, and I asked, "Well, what do you think I should eat?"

My sister said, "I'm going to get a Belgian waffle."

Just the name, Belgian waffles, sounded so exotic, a delicacy from a far-off place. I said, "I'm going to get that, too!"

Just the day before, my breakfast had been some lumpy oatmeal. Earlier that week it'd been powdered eggs. I would've been handed a nearly expired milk carton that had black and brown slivers of something floating in it that was clearly not milk. *Are you for real? You mean, I can order whatever I want?* I felt like I was dreaming, like I hadn't fully awakened in that moment.

The server brought out our Belgian waffles and they looked perfectly fine. I was completely floored when my sister said,

"Let me pose like you do." My sister always tried to make my experience in prison lighter. Visits galvanized me and made me feel like I could get through another week.

"This is burnt." Now sure, the underside was a little charred. And maybe a little bit more than charred, but the top was light and, to my mind, totally edible. But my sister wasn't having it. She called over the server and asked, "Hey, can you make this over? It's burnt."

My face must have registered my shock at the audacity of her request. "Hey, Ace..."

My sister, Aisha, is my number one. We are best friends. She is a year and a half older than me, and I'd always loved hanging out with her and her friends, learning what it meant to be cool.

I was already what elders called an *old soul*. A bit more mature, beyond my years. So hanging out with my older sister seemed normal for me. I'd question her and her friends about girls and they were always cool, saying, "Oh yeah, we'll let you know. We got you!" Ace would give me input on my style. Just a little, here and there. I had a pair of jeans I designed not too long before being arrested. There was a likeness of Big Daddy Kane on the knee and all kinds of colorful art and patches. My sister added, "Oh, if you add this, or flip the patch diagonally, that'll put you over the top." And I did it. She even took some ice and a needle and pierced my ear, which, in the late '80s, only amplified my cool factor. Hanging with her gave me access to little nuggets of teen wisdom that would take me to the next level.

"Ace...all you had to do was scrape that off. In prison—"

But I stopped myself. I wasn't in prison anymore.

If you were a prisoner and then you become a returned citizen, for you to have even a peanut butter and jelly sandwich feels like an enormous privilege. If you have tuna fish with actual mayonnaise, you feel like you're eating a gourmet meal from a Michelin-starred chef.

Unfortunately for this restaurant, they made the choice to take my sister's plate to the kitchen, scrape off the bottom, and return the same waffle back to her. Wrong move! Aisha was livid, and her response was 100 percent New York. She said, "This is not okay! I'm a paying patron. I need to be able to get what I paid for. *This* is unacceptable." And with that they went back and they made it right.

That's when it hit me: *Wow, I'm home. I'm actually free.* In prison, you cower. You accept. You bend. You say, "Oh, somebody spit on that side of the plate? Okay, cool. I'll just eat from the other side." You see a piece of hair? You say, "Oh, let me just carve around that strand. I'll eat the rest." You certainly do not say, "Excuse me, waiter. There's hair in my food." So, in that moment, when I watched my sister demand to be treated fairly, I knew I was home. Not only had my physical self been returned to society, but in many ways, my dignity was also restored. The humanity that was wrongly stripped away from me had been given back.

My mom, sister, and I in Clinton. Visits had a rejuvenating power, and my family would come every visitors' weekend.

There is a saying in prison often used when a person is preparing to be released or their release day is coming up. It's called "getting short." Some of the men would say to me, "Hey, Yusef, you getting short, ain't you?" It means that one's time in the facility is dwindling. In a larger sense, "getting short" is a way of acknowledging that someone is going back into the world. For many reasons, this is cause for both celebration and trepidation.

Prison is its own world. In this created world, so much is normalized. It's normal to hoard your favorite snacks. I loved bean pies but you couldn't get those all the time, so they were definitely treasured. From the commissary, my go-to was Little Debbie Oatmeal Creme Pies. I haven't had them in a long time, but even now, as I write this, I can recall their delicious taste and soft texture. I loved Chips Ahoy! cookies, which were everyone's favorite in the youth facility. Whenever we had an opportunity to use the microwave, people would heat up the chewy ones until they were soft and gooey. It was like being a child all over again, a momentary escape into our lives before.

It's normal for photographs to become your most cherished and protected possession in prison. People could take anything from you but not your photographs, because it felt like stealing your memories, your reminders of freedom. They felt even more important or real than a letter, a way to let your mind escape the confines of prison, to see the people and places you love with your own eyes. Stealing a photograph would be a reason to fight. If we'd been allowed to have a safe or a vault, the photos would have lived in there.

It was also normal to walk in particular ways so that you weren't attacked. You had to keep your head up, keep a steely gaze and a strong chin. You had to watch your back. Never allow yourself to be caught slipping. Awareness of who was standing behind or beside you was paramount. It was normal to align yourself with various groups for protection. It was normal to accept dehumanization in a myriad of forms. Such as being herded like dogs from one part of the jail to the next. The abnormal is made normal, and so it takes time to adjust to the real world and to survive it when you return home. This is why so many men and women have difficulty transitioning back to regular life, and recidivism is incredibly high in some communities. People become acclimated to prison life, and often they aren't given the tools and resources—the actual rehabilitation needed—in order to survive on the outside.

Malcolm X said, "The prison systems in this country actually are exploitative and they are not in any way rehabilitative." Sadly, it's often incumbent upon the person to educate him- or herself while inside. Many states have even been slowly removing education in the prisons, though there are still some facilities that offer vocational and academic training. Sure, there are people who leave prison with tried-and-true skills. I've seen guys go in and learn how to become expert tailors. Others become certified drug counselors. The problem is, when they leave prison, they are unable to sustain their practical needs long enough to be able to put those skills to good use. If they don't have family support, they have to first find housing, and shelters are often crowded and filled with opportunities that scream recidivism. Both rental and job applications can ask for a criminal background check, which leaves them unable to go into the field they trained for. And unfortunately, there are still large numbers of people who leave prison without any education, formal or otherwise, and who have difficulty finding meaning in society. They haven't been holistically trained to live fully independent lives.

There is also another, significant burden on the men and women released from prison: They aren't psychosocially accepted; they aren't seen as persons of value. With that societal judgment and internal struggle compounding the external ones of housing, food, and employment, especially after they had become so acclimated to prison life, they cannot appreciate their value; they do not see themselves as a person born with any real purpose. The world is telling them a lie, and everything they encounter from the time they exist inside those prison walls affirms it. Opening themselves up to the idea that God might use their experience for their good feels foolhardy. Guys have all but said to me that they feel like they were born in error. As a result, they move through life like they are mistakes. And that mentality manifests alongside the choices they make: the ones that send them back to the only place where they believed they had some worth, even if it is a machine whose value system is dehumanizing and distorted.

I'm beyond grateful that while I did struggle for a season with finding ways to live a fully independent life post-release and pre-exoneration, I was ultimately able to find my way.

Kevin and I at our college graduation in the prison yard. We're here with our mothers and our early teacher Helena Nomsa Brath, who taught us in her home while we were on bail. This day felt like a real celebration: We could call ourselves college graduates, we were making something of ourselves, and we weren't letting this scar on our lives shape us.

While imprisoned, I was able to take advantage of some of the programs at Harlem Valley and Clinton. I finished high school as well as completed an associate's degree from Dutchess Community College. Here's the real kicker: Separate from the academic programs, there were some lower-level skill and personal development programs that required we do some counseling. Because I was placed in a unit for those convicted of sex crimes, this often meant sitting down with someone and demonstrating your ability to be accountable for your actions. A unit administrator in a group session would say, "Yusef, you've been a bit quiet lately. Let's talk about your crime. Why are you here?"

"I'm here because of an evil justice system."

They'd press me more, but I held fast to my truth. The coordinator would get frustrated because they couldn't seem to get me to break.

"Okay, Yusef. Tell us how you might consider making amends for your actions," they'd say. I would continue running down the facts of the case as I knew them.

"Look, man, I didn't do this crime. They know I didn't do this crime. We were set up. We are only here because of the politics of the system.

"First of all, how could we have done this if none of those false confessions made any sense? Nobody's alleged confession matched."

And then, "Nobody had any blood on them! None! But they say this lady lost three-fourths of her..."

And obviously, those exchanges didn't always end well. I was kicked out of many sessions and often barred from participating going forward. However, because of the favor I'd garnered with some of those same administrators who I think really believed I was innocent, I didn't experience some of the repercussions other people did. Mr. Shawn Ashby, one of the administrators I'd won over, would simply say, "Okay, Yusef. Just stay in the cell and read."

"Word? I can stay in my cell and read? This is wonderful. No problem. I got my own library." I had a cassette player that allowed me to listen to audiobooks on tape.

Getting my GED at Spofford—before I went to Harlem Valley. Even though the course of my life changed in ways I could never have imagined, I was able to get my GED around the same time that I would have graduated from LaGuardia High School.

I felt deeply for the people I knew who were struggling with all the forms of so-called rehabilitation that were offered. Who, for many valid reasons, couldn't access tools for personal development and as a result firmly identified with prison culture. Nobody actually wants that for themselves.

As my time was getting short, I grew increasingly nervous. The attachments made in prison are very real. The familial nature and the bonds we create with one another are deep. They offer a kind of grounding that allows us to carry on from day to day. I became very close to Abdur Rashid, a Muslim brother who later became my head of security within our community. In prison, some groups were allowed their own kind of government that was honored and respected by the facility. Some communities like ours were faith-based but nevertheless were recognized by the prison. We even had a constitution that governed how we'd operate. As someone who became a leader in the Muslim community—essentially, head of our organization—I was given a right-hand man who was primarily responsible for making sure I was safe. Abdur Rashid would walk with me when I'd go minister to inmates in other units and make sure no one would run up on me or attack me.

Abdur and I were from totally different worlds but became great friends. It wasn't like we were just two guys in prison together—you go to your cell and I go to mine. We'd meet in the prayer room and say, "What's up, Brother? What are some of your ideas?" Abdur was a warrior but also someone who was eager to learn. We had both a spiritual and an intellectual connection. We created a program for our community called The Meeting of the Minds, which allowed us to minister to our brothers in a separate space in the prison. They even let us paint the wall, which was unheard of. Because of my artistic background, I wanted more than black letters on a white wall. No, we used calligraphy and bright, bold images. The wall transformed into something so colorful and expressive. We needed that. It was our space, and getting a chance to make it feel welcoming was humanizing. In that space, we were free to think, operate, and respect one another. We treated each other with value and really got a chance to understand each other. That was another thing I appreciated about Islam, especially in prison. Yeah, you got protection, but we were more about making sure that you felt human again. Like you were sane. Like thriving was possible inside of a place that was trying to kill anything beautiful inside of us.

Abdur Rashid sent me this photo of himself a few years after he was released, and I was still inside. He had reinvented himself, moved from Rochester to Atlanta and away from an environment that could have pulled him back into his old life. He went on to work in the music industry and became a video content creator.

Our bond in that space was one of intimate friendship. We all wanted to hold on to those relationships for dear life. Everyone had their own pods or cliques. Certain people were closer to each other than others. And many brothers would do anything to hold on to one another inside. So, I'd heard about people doing terrible things to make sure someone wouldn't go home. All because they wanted that person to stay, for those bonds to remain unbroken. On the far end of the spectrum, particularly in an adult facility, you could be hurt or killed. One guy, who'd gone to parole and thought he lost (he hadn't) was so angry and upset that he went to the bathroom and happened upon someone he had beef with. Both men had razors, and they ended up slicing each other up horribly. The pain of wanting to leave, yet also wanting to stay, was too much.

Bottom line: If folks found out you were leaving too early, you could be assaulted. People would set you up so you might stay in a little longer. Anything could happen.

While a release date is never publicly announced in prison, everyone knows when a person's time is getting short because they start giving stuff away. If you have a black-and-white TV, which some people did, or a stockpile of snacks, you slowly but surely start distributing them to the people around you. So because my name was known in the prison—due to the public nature of the case but also because of the reputation I'd attained as a spiritual leader—I had to be very careful about how I donated my possessions. I had books, a few prayer rugs, and a black-and-white television, which was a really big deal. I did not plan to take most of it home. I began to carefully distribute my things to a few select men under the radar. I didn't want to alert the masses and experience any of the trouble that would bring. It didn't feel like I was being released from prison; it felt like I was escaping. Of course, I didn't belong there, and I had always felt that, too.

∾

There are two ways to escape prison. There is, of course, the physical withdrawal. Even legitimate releases can feel very much like a kind of extrication as your body has become so used to the routines and machinations of prison life. But escape happens in other ways as well. The second version of escape can happen from day one. We can escape mentally. And that was my intention from the moment I arrived.

Escaping from prison mentally allows for freedom even when one's body is in bondage. To mentally unlock the chain that's wrapped around your mind once those cell doors shut behind you. So you can still dream! You can still plan! You think and imagine yourself in a better situation. Just like a modern-day vision board, your mind becomes a place of liberation. A place where you can create a reality for yourself that's different from the one you are experiencing. A reality that, if you are released, can be re-created. But it cannot be realized if you don't know who you are.

၄၁

My growth in the first years of prison was exponential. Self-knowledge and self-awareness were on my prison syllabus, for sure. When I was in prison, a simple but most profound question was asked of me: "Who are you?"

Six months into my bid, Jerome Jones, a corrections officer, asked me, "Who are you?"

I answered as a teenager trying to parse the magnitude of

what had just happened to me. "I'm Yusef Salaam, one of the guys they accused of raping the Central Park jogger, but I didn't do it."

Jerome replied, "I know that. I've been watching you. You're not supposed to be here. Who are you?"

This second probing confused me. I said, "Oh, shucks. I don't know." But in that moment, something shifted inside me. It occurred to me that I actually *didn't* know who I was. Sure, I was the son of Sharonne Salaam, brother of Shareef and Aisha, but who was *I*? And that began my long spiritual and personal journey of realizing who and why I am. I would lie in my cell and ask myself, *Why was I born? What am I supposed to contribute to this world? Why am I going through this?* But these were questions and not laments. That curiosity became the driver for every choice I made while in prison. Every book I read. The work I did to keep up with school.

This was how I chose to approach doing time. Knowing I was innocent, even having these correctional officers affirm my innocence, and still feeling helpless to do anything about my physical incarceration could have driven me mad. No one would have faulted me if it had. But because of the foundation my mother had given and my growing faith at the time, I decided to become an active creator in my own mental freedom. I would sit in my cell and create imprints on my mind of what it was I wanted in the future. I pictured myself free, and I held on to that picture for dear life. I found that your imagination is a precursor of what is to come, what's possible.

Now, in my work as a motivational speaker, the terminology has changed a bit. I'm no longer asking, "Why did I go through that?" I'm asking, "How did I *grow* through that?" I'm walking out my purpose now, carrying with me a story that's impactful and a magnanimity toward the injustice I experienced, so that I now feel a responsibility to those who come into my orbit. I see myself, because of my experience, as a caretaker of people's souls.

This is a critical lesson from my life that I want to share. Whatever imprisons you in one area doesn't have any control over your mind. Poor health, poverty, and lack of support, to name some examples, are all very real burdens. As real as my body in prison. And many of these issues are the function of grave, systemic injustices that absolutely need to be examined and reckoned with. We *must* keep working together for change, whether it be by making donations, protesting, refusing to stay silent, calling legislators, or using whatever means we choose to do this work. But alongside all of this, what's also important is that you envision a future for yourself, and not allow these injustices to dictate what that vision is. So, you're a freshman college student feeling imprisoned by a lack of understanding or support from family? Meditate on the affirmation "I'm going to graduate." Visualize yourself taking that tassel and moving it from one side of your head to the other. Marry that vision with a feeling of what it will be like to be in that room: the cheers, everyone excited by their sense of achievement, the room vibrating with the palpable hope of what is to come, the joy of being celebrated by your friends and your family—the people who tried their best, within their own capacities, to be there for you. Do that visualization daily, weekly, whenever sorrow and despair try to take over. You'll smile because you will have acknowledged all that you've endured, that all your experiences have brought you to where you are. You are on purpose. You are on assignment.

In prison, I saw myself as a free person. I visualized myself being able to walk down 125th Street in Harlem with my big LL Cool J boom box, pumping some reggae music and maybe even visiting Mart 125 or Dr. J's. I visualized stopping by my friend Muhammad's store, Muhatino's, to get one of his dope hats that hip hop artists like Queen Latifah and Kool Moe Dee would wear. I visualized even maybe finally speaking to Julie Dash, the director of the critically acclaimed film *Daughters of the Dust*, who happened to live in my building. I would lie in bed at night and ponder whether these places and people were going to be the same when I got back, or what had changed. My mother would send me photographs of the neighborhood, so I could see the changes and the old places. These visions and affirmations helped sustain me.

This reminds me of some of the narratives written by enslaved Africans and slaveholders. When a slaver would come to examine the "product" and saw someone who stood out, they might say, "Wow! Look at that one." It was usually because the person looked regal and confident even on an auction block or a sales floor. The buyer would turn and say, "I want that one," and the seller would reply, "Oh no, that one is not for sale." The buyer would ask, "Why?" and the seller would respond with, "That one was a prince and he knows it!" He never forgot who he was. He buried that knowledge inside himself, and it radiated outward.

Me and Kevin, together in brotherhood. We did time separately, even though we were in the same facility, but we were eventually in the college unit together. In this photo I'm wearing one of the many T-shirts I created and designed myself. I would lay down Scotch tape over a shirt and draw my design with a pencil. Then, using a tiny pin, I would cut out a part of the tape, peel it off, and paint the shirt. The Scotch tape acted as a template, and this became my version of silk-screening.

That was what I had to do in prison. I knew I was innocent. I knew I was born on purpose and with a purpose. To survive, I did my best to follow the rules in prison. But on the inside, I never forgot who I was. I buried that knowledge inside myself and let my mind paint an alternative picture to the one I was living.

Consider this as a way of navigating those difficult days. Because life will certainly challenge you. Life will sometimes even run you over. But the power of your comeback lies in what you allow yourself to think, the thoughts you allow to marinate.

I want you to know that, yes, your time is getting short. Your release from whatever imprisons you is coming. Embrace it. Go into stealth mode and start giving away those things you don't need. Give away that self-doubt. Trash those insecurities. Set your mind free, and when you finally are able to breathe fresh air, tell your story. You, too, can look at your life and see a higher purpose. There are certainly evil and ignorant people in this world who have codified a reality that is to your detriment. They have created cages in order to create animals so they'll have an excuse to create more cages. But we all have the power to blossom behind those bars.

TWO

Master Yusef Salaam

If I'm gonna tell a real story, I'm gonna start with my name.

KENDRICK LAMAR

An early photo of me with my flattop and a Black Bart and Maggie Simpson.

MAIL FOR YUSEF SALAAM!"

Her voice was surprisingly warm. Like syrup on pancakes or a cozy throw blanket on a cool autumn day. When we think about correctional officers, we often imagine burly, rough men and hardened women. And in some cases, especially in an adult facility, those stereotypes are not far from the truth. But in the youth facility, Ms. Eleanore Faulkner was a balm for all of us. Her skin, a smooth dark brown, reminded me of my own. She wore her glasses on the tip of her nose like a librarian, and when she put those letters in my hand, she'd smile. It was a simple thing, her cheerfulness. But it encouraged me, and all of us there. Especially in the midst of the seemingly insurmountable obstacles we all were facing. All our mail was prescreened for contraband, and her smile was the grounding force we needed before we picked up our violated envelopes and packages.

For me, Ms. Eleanore's acknowledgment of my humanity was supported by the name that would appear on every letter my grandmother would send to me. My grandmother loved to constantly send me those Blue Mountain cards with the lyrical prose meant to comfort and reassure the receiver. She would address them to:

MASTER YUSEF SALAAM

I suspect that this was her way of reminding me of who I was. When I looked up the noun *master*, I read things like "a man in charge," "a skilled practitioner," and "a man of high rank." No matter how the criminal justice system and media tried to frame me with the horrifying narrative they'd expertly crafted about me and the others, and no matter how anyone else chose to see me, my grandmother, prophetically, wrote into existence who she knew me to be. Above and beyond the emotional and psychological impact of seeing my name written that way, I also believe that my Mommie—that's what we called my grandmother—was strategic. She was seed-planting. She also wanted the correctional officers to know who they were holding. To insulate me from any harm that could have come my way from either their hands or their neglect. She wanted them to know there were people outside of that facility who loved and cherished me. That I was worthy of being cared for. In her own way, she was laying the foundation of a mental and emotional fence with just three simple words.

I never got a chance to ask her why she did that. She lost her ability to speak after having a stroke, and she passed away in 2014. But I know it was her clandestine way of sending me a message of confidence. Like the stories of people sending coded secret messages in letters during the World Wars, in the way

Even toward the end of her life, after suffering multiple strokes, my grandmother still exuded moments of regalness. One day we were in a cab together going toward my mom's apartment, and at this point she had lost her speech. As we pulled up, she said, clear as day, "Pay the man." But even when she couldn't speak, she would express her excitement and joy. There was a loving fullness to her gaze. She would look at me in a way that clearly said, "That's my grandson, the one I call Master Yusef Salaam."

she addressed her letters to me, my Mommie was telling me to straighten my back. She was telling me that I was a master of my faith. She was telling me that this should not define me and that I was bigger than the box they wanted to put me in. And I took those "secret" messages to heart. I became the Master of my fate, even behind bars.

∽

There's power in a name. Even more than the name itself, there's power in the name you answer to. Those two things intersect in many ways, I've learned. Writer Mia Sogoba writes in her essay, "The Power of a Name":

> In West African culture, many factors are at work in the naming process and a seemingly simple name can hold someone's entire biography. A West African name is much more than a simple, functional tag to identify someone. It is a symbol, an emblem.
>
> A name can shape a person's character, mold their social identity, and even influence their destiny. The meaning attached to a name will determine much about the present and the future of a child.

I would learn this to be true about my own name. But first, I needed to know the names of One greater than me.

I remember a day early on in the trial when I was going back and forth between court and the youth facility. A man came up to me, said he was Muslim, and greeted me. That wasn't so strange. I'd encountered many different people as we traveled back and forth from Spofford to the courthouse. Some people would offer words of encouragement and support. Others would spew hatred, like when a white guy pointed his fingers at me as if he were squeezing the trigger of a gun. It could go either way.

Nevertheless, this man was different. I was startled by what he said: "Your father gave me this book for you." Mind you, I was fifteen years old, and I hadn't seen or talked to my father since I was four. This man pressed the book into my hands. It was *The 99 Beautiful Names of Allah*, and I still have it to this day. What was interesting about the text was that it was framed as a book of prescriptions—yes, like medical prescriptions. The implication was that within the 99 names of the Creator, you could find a remedy for whatever ailed you. For instance, if you were sick, you would call on one of His names from the Faith, Shafi. Shafi is the Healer, and you could say, "Ya, Shafi, oh Healer, heal me. I need Your help."

As confused as I was that my absent father sent me the book through a stranger, I do consider it a cherished offering for the journey I was on. It was my first encounter with the power of naming, and it would not be my last. I would soon confront my own name and its meaning.

Salaam is one of the names of God/Allah. Muslims, because they're not allowed to call themselves by the names of Allah, will often put Abdul, Abdur, or Abdus before the name of God to distinguish themselves from the mighty Creator. While it's not what's on my birth certificate, in my faith tradition, my name is Yusef Abdus Salaam.

So when Jerome Jones, the corrections officer, asked me that question, "Who are you?" I didn't know where to begin the journey of finding out. Yet the question opened my mind and, in a way, gave me permission to start the process of self-discovery. And what better place to start than the beginning? With my name.

My father brought Islam to our family, and my mother converted immediately afterward. I was born into a Muslim household, and so we didn't have baby showers celebrating a child prior to their birth. In Islamic tradition, parents were to observe the baby for seven days and then name the child based on what they saw. On the seventh day, my parents called family and friends to the baby-naming ceremony and pronounced me to be Yusef Idris Faadel Abdus Salaam.

But growing up, I never knew what my name meant. My mother and father likely knew, but I never asked. Understanding the origins of my name and ultimately what they might have "observed" in those seven days became a starting point to answering Jerome's pivotal question. I began diving into book after book, finding out, in one instance, that the Arabic equivalent in English of the name Yusef is Joseph. Joseph/Yusuf/Yusef means "God will increase." The literal meaning that I found in one book said, "He enlarges." Meaning God enlarges, increases, makes bigger.

This of course led me to the biblical Joseph, who is also Yusuf (ع) in the Qur'an. This is where the prophetic nature of our naming traditions began to reveal itself.

Joseph/Yusuf (ع) was the dream interpreter who was placed in charge of the pharaoh's palace. But he did not start out that way. Before that, he was in prison. And prior to prison, his brothers, in their jealousy, had wanted to kill him. But then they said, "Let's not kill him. Let's put him in the well. Hopefully, somebody will pick him up and he'll be done with." And sure enough, Joseph/Yusuf (ع) was put in the well. But he was also rescued, though it didn't look pretty. He was taken as a slave. And despite that, he did not die. It was not his time to die. Later, after being falsely accused of sexual assault, he was placed in prison.

Pharaoh sent for Joseph, and he was quickly brought from the dungeon. When he had shaved and changed his clothes, he came before Pharaoh.

Pharaoh said to Joseph, "I had a dream, and no one can interpret it. But I have heard it said of you that when you hear a dream you can interpret it."

"I cannot do it," Joseph replied to Pharaoh, "but God will give Pharaoh the answer he desires...

"It is just as I said to Pharaoh: God has shown Pharaoh what he is about to do. Seven years of great abundance are coming throughout the land of Egypt, but seven years of famine will follow them. Then all the abundance in Egypt will be forgotten, and the famine will ravage the land. The abundance in the land will not be remembered, because the famine that follows it will be so severe. The reason the dream was given to Pharaoh in two forms is that the matter has been firmly decided by God, and God will do it soon.

"And now let Pharaoh look for a discerning and wise man and put him in charge of the land of Egypt. Let Pharaoh appoint commissioners over the land to take a fifth of the harvest of Egypt during the seven years of abundance. They should collect all the food of these good years that are coming and store up the grain under the authority of Pharaoh, to be kept in the cities for food. This food should be held in reserve for the country, to be used during the seven years of famine that will come upon Egypt, so that the country may not be ruined by the famine."

The plan seemed good to Pharaoh and to all his officials. So Pharaoh asked them, "Can we find anyone like this man, one in whom is the spirit of God?"

Then Pharaoh said to Joseph, "Since God has made all this known to you, there is no one so discerning and wise as you. You shall be in charge of my palace, and all my people are to submit to your orders. Only with respect to the throne will I be greater than you."

Genesis 41:14–16, 28–40 (NIV)

As the story reveals, Joseph/Yusuf (ﷻ) was divinely released from captivity there as well. He would later become governor of all Egypt and a great prophet.

My sixteen-year-old mind was completely blown! I couldn't believe what I was reading. I felt like I was unraveling my whole story; my destiny was unfolding right in front of me in these sacred texts.

In Yusuf's (ﷻ) story in the Qur'an, it states that Joseph's brothers didn't know who they had. The prison guards didn't know who they had. I would argue that maybe even Joseph didn't know who they had. His identity was revealed to him through these miraculous rescues.

More than forty years ago, my parents observed me for seven days and gave me a name that divinely aligned with my journey.

As I read the story of Yusuf (ﷻ) in the Qur'an and Joseph in the Bible, I received spiritual nourishment. Over and over I said, *Wow, Allah is talking to me.* I appreciated that divine nod. I don't believe myself to be a modern-day Yusuf (ﷻ), but reading those stories and connecting them to my own helped me realize that Allah's miracles have not stopped. Sitting in my jail cell at sixteen years old, I learned that I was a miracle waiting to happen. The uncovering of who I was required me to use my choices to participate in that miracle in a meaningful way. Every day I had a chance to push that miracle forward to fruition. I also somehow understood that even when names are forgotten, the justice and reality of God/Allah remains. The time I spent unpacking my first name was also the first time I said to myself, *This is Allah's doing. Allah is allowing this to become a beautiful story, as opposed to the tragedy some people intended.*

It wasn't too long after reading these sacred texts that I wrote the following poem:

In between Venus and Mars
Is the center of our attraction
Of those connected to the stars
Hardly a fraction
It behooves man to work for the day
when this will all end
Life is mortal, so follow the way of those heaven sent
Awaken and receive that which will give you life
Or remain horizontal and never begin the flight
For the solution, I'll descend from amongst the stars
And I'll meet you between Venus and Mars.

There I was, in the Dannemora prison, walking to the mess hall, and these words came pouring into and out of me. I remember saying, "Somebody give me a napkin!" and I wrote and wrote until I couldn't anymore. I knew it wasn't my words. I knew that the Creator was speaking to me. I was just a vessel. It was like the revelation of my name had awakened something in me. In my writing of that poem, more of my identity was being revealed.

More digging led me to the meaning of Idris, my middle name. Idris is the Arabic equivalent to the prophet Enoch in the Bible, and the name means "teacher." Faadel means "with justice." And Salaam is a name for God/Allah and means *"the Owner and Source of all Peace."* So at sixteen years old, six months into a prison bid for a crime I didn't commit, and after the prompting of a guard who saw "something" in me I couldn't yet see, I learned for the first time that my name meant: "God will increase the teacher with justice and peace."

Whew!

The truth is, I was always Yusef Idris Faadel Salaam. Even before the accusation, the trial, and prison. I was this person before I even had a tangible hold on what it meant to be that person. But it was almost as if the moment I learned my name's meaning was the right time, that I was ready to know it without any doubt. At that moment, with a future that looked bleak, I was ready to understand everything that would happen going forward. I was ready to see the miracle of my life unfold.

In hindsight, I'm certain I wasn't the only one who was beginning to see who I was, who I'd always been. I remember being in the youth facility and coming into my cell after being in some other part of the building only to find Tropicana orange juice and Entenmann's cookies on my bed. When it first happened, it felt like a mirage. I thought maybe I was just longing for the luxuries of home. I kept thinking, *Am I tripping?* But then I realized that the cookies and juice were real, and I heard my mother's voice in my head saying, *I was raised in the Jim Crow South.* In other words: Be suspicious.

I said, "Man, they're trying to kill me with the food. I'm not eating that."

But once again, bless the kind heart of Ms. Eleanore Faulkner. One day she came up to me and said, "Have you been getting the goodies I've been leaving in your cell?"

"Oh wow! Wow. Yes. Why did you leave those for me?"

She said, "Yusef, I know you're not supposed to be here, but I can't take this key and let you go. Every time I come here, I want to make your time as easy and as sweet as possible. That's why I bring these things and leave them for you."

Whoa.

She saw me. *Really* saw me. I don't think she knew the meaning of my name, but God/Allah used her to protect and shield me. To rescue this Yusef from the destruction others intended.

❧

This discussion of names reminds me of Kunta Kinte in Alex Haley's *Roots*. We read of a man who was told his name was Toby, and he refused to accept it. "No, my name is Kunta," he said, holding tightly to his name, to his heritage, to the last vestiges of freedom. And there were consequences for his resistance. The slave masters whipped him mercilessly until he submitted to this new name and a new "story" of himself. But he didn't really submit. We have Haley's *Roots* because Kunta only pretended to accept this false narrative. In the miniseries adaptation, we hear Kunta's resolve: "They can put the chains on your body. Never let them put the chains on your mind." In order to live, to survive for his children and his children's children, he chose to hold on to the knowledge of who he was and where he'd come from and bury it deep inside himself.

I suppose that's what many of us have to do. In order to survive, to live another day, we have to bury the truth while taking the narratives given to us. The systems and institutions around us make this necessary at times. However, the biggest challenge we face is in not forgetting what we buried. We cannot forget. We must keep the constant reminders of our inherent value in our lives—even when we can't announce it to the world. If we don't, we will end up buying into the lies about who we are. Those letters my grandma sent were my reminders. That book my father gave me was a reminder. Unfortunately, many of the young boys and men I was imprisoned alongside had forgotten.

If we are to have any success, however that's defined, we must hold on to the truth of who we are. We must fully embrace the power of our names, and the power of the name we answer to.

We should ask all the questions, we must—and believe me, I have. Why are there so many Black and Brown bodies incarcerated? Why is there a clear and concerted effort to ensure we occupy jails more than we occupy college campuses? Why would our government pay upward of $200,000 to house juveniles as opposed to using half of that money to offer us alternatives to improve our lives and the lives of our families? The answers have been expertly unpacked in documentaries, such as *13th* by Ava DuVernay, and in books like *The New Jim Crow* by Michelle Alexander. Alexander even gave us a crystal clear characterization of it all: "Many of the forms of discrimination that relegated African Americans to an inferior caste during Jim Crow continue to apply to huge segments of the black population today—provided they are first labeled felons."

But if we were to dig even deeper than the systems and structures, I think we'd find what we always find at the heart of white supremacy: the mission to get Black people to believe the definitions they have of us, to narrate our lives in such a way that it actually affirms the false notions of inferiority, in order to trap us in a system where we simply become mindless cogs in the wheels of Western capitalism.

Newton's third law of motion states that for every action there's an equal and opposite reaction, and that certainly applies when discussing the issue of crime and poverty within Black and Brown communities. Many people are examining and dissecting the myth of Black-on-Black crime. And it's important to note the word *myth* because statistically most crimes occur within one's own ethnic group. But if crime in some of our communities is prevalent, it's mostly due to systems that have perpetuated poverty in these communities and ensured the pervasiveness of racism. It's imperative to view these things as a reaction to something that was set into motion long ago, to look at the actions that produced these reactions. The behaviors and intentions at the foundation of white supremacy created a criminal justice system that would do everything in its ample power to wrongly imprison five teenage boys, to essentially change our names and the trajectories of our lives. Our options were limited and clear to us even back then: If we buy into their narratives of who we are, then we can never survive outside the construct they built. If we don't, then they'll attempt to destroy our lives.

But I refused.

They could accuse me of rape. They could convict me of rape. They could whip me mercilessly in the press. But thanks to my courageous mother, my praying grandmother, and a village full of support, they could never get me to truly believe I was that person. I would never accept the construct they were trying to build for me.

Never.

THREE

Before

He was only seventeen, in a madman's dream
The cops shot the kid, I still hear him scream.

SLICK RICK

In first grade at P.S. 83.

THERE'S A LONG LIST OF all the ways in which injustice has stolen things from my life. I prefer, however, to remember all I've been able to hold. Ever since I was a kid, I've always had mad love for hip hop, and at one point I'd wanted a career as a rap artist. My mother never really liked the genre, mostly because she couldn't understand what they were saying. She never discouraged me from following my dreams, though. Her only advice to me in regard to my career ambitions was this: "Talk slow enough for people to understand what you're saying. Don't mumble." I took her advice to heart. I believed I had important things to say, and that it was important I say them in a way that would increase the impact on the listener.

I was a decent student, but the arts were my first love. In New York, riding the trains and buses to get to school was normal. My mom trusted me to get to school safe and on time, even though I had to travel to Lincoln Center, farther away from my neighborhood than most. It's funny to think about how even though I was only twelve years old, I was a student at LaGuardia High School of Music and Art. I was in high school a year and a half earlier than I was supposed to be because my mother had started me in kindergarten early. Like many mothers, she had to work outside the home, and so, because nobody really checked those things back then, she enrolled me in school when I was three and a half. It also helped that I was always tall for my age.

LaGuardia was such a different world, but I fit in perfectly. It was a liberating place. Many of the students would go on to become famous actors and comedians. Omar Epps, Marlon Wayans, and Carl Anthony Payne from *The Cosby Show* all went there, and I got a chance to see so much talent in one place. My previous school had been so different. There were regular classes, bland state-issued curricula and texts, and maybe a few after-school activities. But LaGuardia felt like the world to me. I was one of the visual arts students and we were always creating. You'd walk down the hall and see choreographers working on a movement. And that was it: Everyone was always creating, and I soaked all of that in.

We were all artistic dreamers making plans to live out our creative futures as singers, dancers, painters, actors. Again, it was New York. What better place to do exactly that? I was going to be a rapper, so I decided to take the first step toward making things happen. At that time, ASCAP (the American Society of Composers, Authors and Publishers) was up the block from my school. They had rap applications back then. You could fill out one to become a songwriter.

"I'm going to do it!"

I went up to the floor where ASCAP was located. I picked

up my rap application and stared at the lines and information. Then I got cold feet. I never filled it out, never turned it in.

I think everyone has that moment when we hesitate right before attempting something that feels significant. Sometimes it's fear of the unknown. Other times it's doubt. In hindsight, doubt might be why I hesitated and didn't return the application. If we could learn not to doubt ourselves and just execute, we would be so much more on top of what we are trying to achieve. But everybody has their moment, and that was mine. The worst part about it is that you can never get that moment back.

Even now, I sometimes wonder what would have happened if I did. Would the trajectory of my life have been different? Would I have been the next LL or Nas? Who knows? Nevertheless, I still wrote and practiced my lyrics. I still wanted to be a rapper.

Hip hop culture wasn't just about the music, though. It was a lifestyle. It was the dope beats, but it was also the fly clothes, shoes, and accessories. There was a way rappers moved that conveyed confidence bordering on arrogance. They lived on that fine line; it was how they drew us into their world wholesale. Hip hop was just as much LL's Kangol as it was his words. When he spit, "Terrorizing my neighbors with the heavy bass / I keep the suckers in fear by the look on my face," we wanted a taste of that fury. Two generations later they would call it swag. We called it fresh. Hip hop was MC Lyte's flow, but it was also the asymmetric haircut that all the girls rocked. It was the black leather outfits Kool Moe Dee wore. It was the African medallions worn by all the so-called "gods" in the game.

During my time at LaGuardia High School. In 2010, I ran into my old friend Serena (in the hat) at a protest during our fight with the City of New York for a settlement. She came up to me and we embraced, reunited after all these years.

I loved it all.

As an earnest dreamer who also happened to be a Black boy growing up in Harlem, I was aware of all the dangers that lurked in the city. For a while there, none of those dangers affected me. I flowed in and out of all the boroughs, dressed in my Triple F.A.T. Goose, my kufi or crown, and my medallions without a second thought. I took shortcuts through tunnels and never had a problem.

That is, until one day I encountered the Decepticons. They were New York's most notorious gang. This group of young men traveled fifty-deep and were the most feared crew in the whole city. If they came to your school, everyone was in trouble. One day, they set their sights on LaGuardia High School of Music and Art. Truth be told, they didn't really mess with the Black folks. They targeted white students who had money and nice things. They were coming to get it all.

On the day they came to my school, I had just gotten out and headed to the 1 train at Sixty-Sixth Street and went through the tunnel that put me below Lincoln Center. I walked underneath the street to get to the turnstile area. I could've walked upstairs and gone around instead, which was a longer and safer path, but I didn't feel like there was anything for me to fear.

That day, as I was taking the short route in the middle of the tunnel, the Decepticons turned the corner. I always carried my pocketknife with me. Because I was tall, people thought I was older than I was, and they would haze me. I stayed ready for whatever. My mind went to my knife when I saw them coming but I didn't make any sudden moves.

I was beyond afraid. I wasn't sure if I was shaking on the outside, or if they could smell the fear on me, but I certainly was trembling on the inside. I finally put my hand on my knife and said to myself, *If they take me, I'm taking them.* I wasn't a chump, and I wasn't going to get beat up. Two hundred–plus feet below Lincoln Center, a place where affluence and wealth reigned, lay this jungle made of iron and steel. I knew this wasn't a moment for me to have a bunch of words. This was a moment for me to stand my ground with one look. I couldn't allow them to smell my fear. But still, I was scared. I was wearing what we called "the culture" from head to toe. I had a crown on my head. I had black African medallions. I think I also had on my Rasta belt. All of these adornments were ripe for the taking.

They surrounded me. It felt like they were ravenous wolves, and I was raw meat. All I could see in my mind's eye was my body mangled after they were done with me. Then one of them muttered in Patois, "Nah, him all right…"

They all left.

I don't remember if I ever walked that tunnel again. But I'd gotten their respect. They'd essentially said, "Oh, he's cool."

Nothing else. Four words and they let me be.

This was not how it would usually go. In a very real way, I could have lost my life that day. I could have been stabbed and left to die. In a poem I wrote called "New York-ish," I captured this feeling: "New York will have you on some, eat a cat like a lion, spit the bones out, and beat they soul with it." As a Black boy growing up in a place made a jungle by those who colonized its human resources, this confrontation was familiar. And because I recognized it, I survived it.

Still, for the longest time, I wondered why they didn't do anything to me. Maybe they let me go because I could understand what they were saying to each other. Even as a kid, I'd always been able to pick up accents and dialects easily. The Decepticons were mostly immigrants, speaking Patois. I understood them perfectly. I could understand the nuances of dropped consonants and elongated vowels. I think this is a gift that I've yet to unpack fully—except that God was preparing me to be able to understand a diversity of people, to be able to converse and connect with them at the heart level.

I later learned that they probably left me alone because they didn't think that I was African American. They likely thought I was an African in America, an immigrant. It was such a strange and common phenomenon in New York. Black Americans were often believed to be unworthy of rising to greatness, even by some of our own brothers and sisters from the Diaspora.

They spared my life on that day because they were immigrants who saw themselves as victims here in the United States. When they looked at me, they didn't see raw meat. They saw themselves. They said, "Oh, he's not from here. He's okay. He may be West Indian or this or that." It's funny how because of the Decepticons I started claiming my father's Bajan lineage more. I somehow believed that it was another layer of protection I could wear to keep me safe. But it would take a couple more years for me to realize that, to white folks, Black is Black.

I believe strongly in the spiritual connection of all things. All these moments when I could have died, where I could have been destroyed, taught me that I am supposed to be here, right now, doing everything I'm doing, speaking truth as I've experienced it to the masses. Everything I've witnessed and lived through was necessary in order for me to impart information and direction and guidance. That's what early hip hop did. There was always a message in the music and music in the message. There was always someone telling stories, however embellished, of their journey through life. It was alchemy. Even though I never became a rapper, I still get to do that every day. There's only one person I wish I'd gotten a chance to tell my story to: my father.

∽

My parents got married by the Imam of the large, ornate mosque on Seventy-Second Street on the West Side. My father left our home when I was about four years old.

With the exception of the time he sent me the book on the 99 names of Allah while I was on trial, he never reached out to me. Because of that stark absence, I have only a few memories of him with our family.

Early in my parents' marriage, when I was a toddler, we moved from New York City to Savannah, Georgia. I remember one balmy night, we were all sitting in the house when my father put his fingers to his lips and said, "Shh!" As kids who looked up to this grand figure, we dutifully obeyed.

Dad then grabbed his shotgun, aimed it in the direction of something we could not see, and then BOOM! The whole house shook.

We were stunned by the sound but not afraid. He was our father. If he did it, then it needed to happen, we thought.

It was a mouse.

For a long time, we walked around that hole in the floor of our home.

I don't know why he shot the mouse. Dad didn't explain things. It was simply a given that something was in our home that wasn't allowed and it needed to die. It seemed as if this was just his way of dealing with things. My mother once said, "Your father was the type of man that if you crossed him, he'd spit in your eye and then cut it out." But, maybe because I was a small child and he was my dad, I never saw him that way.

I'm grateful for these flashes of memory, though: I see myself in storefront windows holding his hand. I see my mother's face, frustrated at him. I know they must have been going through

On the rooftop with my parents.

something hard, though I've never had the courage to ask her about it.

My last memory of him is also fleeting. We were in Georgia. It was me, my mother, and my siblings. We were all sitting in one of those old U-Haul trucks with the big front seat. I believe my mother was driving.

She was leaving him. We were going back to New York. Dad was staying down south.

We never saw him after that.

About ten years ago, Aisha got in touch with him, first writing him a letter and then a phone call. He was living in Charleston, South Carolina, by then. He'd had other relationships and other children. When she first told me she'd found him, my heart beat wildly in my chest. I kept saying to myself, *Man, one day I'm going to go see him.* There was a real wanting there. A desire to know this part of me. People used to say we looked almost identical. The elders who knew him would say he "spit me out."

But I never got the chance. He passed away in 2015.

The things I do know about my father are the remnants of stories told by family, mostly my aunt, who was the person on that side who kept track of everything and everybody; she, too, recently passed away. My father had five or six brothers. He was an actor who appeared briefly in the film *Daughters of the Dust*. He was also a photographer. In fact, he met my mother because she was a model and he was a photographer hired for fashion shows.

In 2019, at a convention I was attending in Georgia, a vendor said to me, "I know your father." This guy was about my age.

"Oh wow."

Then he said, "Yeah, your father, he used to work on the ships. He built ships."

That really struck me. My father built ships? Just one more thing I didn't know.

I must admit that not knowing made me feel the loss of not having a relationship with my father even more. Hearing a stranger share this tidbit of information was like, "Damn, my dad has this whole life that we know nothing about and we will never know nothing about." I have siblings I don't know and that just makes that gap, that absence, feel deeper.

My father apparently lived many lives. In Islam, he was considered to be a sage in the community. In Islamic terminology, he was the Sheikh. My father was very rigid in his understanding and practice of Islam, too. My mother told me, "Your father was a brilliant photographer [but after becoming a Muslim] he ripped all of his photos up and destroyed them." In Islam, you're taught that making pictures is considered haram (forbidden). I don't know if it's haram in the same sense as eating pork or murdering someone, but the reason is because they're told that God is the only Creator and on the day of judgment, God will challenge you to give that picture life. It's the same idea that shows up in the Bible about not making graven images.

I no longer carry much anger toward my father and his decision to be absent. It's more of a void. My siblings certainly hold him accountable for the way things went. Aisha would lament that we have an older brother we don't know. That we have younger siblings, either two or three, whom we don't know. There's certainly some regret that I didn't get a chance to connect with him before he died. Mostly, though, it's a deep, abiding longing.

There are days I feel lost when I think about him. There's a tension there. On the one hand, I can spiritually reconcile that my father did all that he had in his capacity to do, and yet on the other, I wonder why he didn't stretch himself a bit more.

What helps me feel just a little less lost is knowing that there's a Creator, that the reality I'm experiencing is temporary. There's a verse in the Qur'an that says, "We awakened them that they might question one another. Said a speaker from among them, 'How long have you remained [here]?' They said, 'We have remained a day or part of a day'" (18:19). "And indeed, a day with your Lord is like a thousand years of those which you count" (22:47). So there is a comfort I have in believing that if my father is accepted into paradise, I'll see him again. And when I want to feel his energy in my presence, I hold his copy of the Qur'an. I kneel on his prayer rug. These were all given to me by my aunt after he passed.

That said, there's never been any part of me that thinks, *If my dad was here, I wouldn't have gone through what I did*, or that things would have happened differently. Even at fifteen and sixteen years old, I was already self-aware enough to know that God is the only One in control.

The flip side of that yearning is that I made a commitment to never cause my children to feel the way I felt. Through divorce and a blended family, I made a pact that my children would always know me. Whether a relationship works or not, that I would always be in their lives. And I've done that. Despite my ex-wife and I no longer being together, I can pull up and see our children anytime. I get immense joy in participating in their lives. And they know how much I love them.

∽

David Nocenti was my Big Brother when I was part of the Big Brothers Big Sisters League of New York in the late '80s. Whenever I think about what it means to have a father figure or an older brother in my life, I think about my uncle Frank and David. David was definitely a big brother in every sense of the name that matters. We hung out together a lot. He took me to

Me at David Nocenti's parents' pool in New Jersey.
My uncle Frank was the one who taught me how to
swim.

the movies and even swimming at his parents' house in New
Jersey. David was also the male role model my mother looked
to in guiding me as a teenager, and he was a critical advocate for
me when I was arrested. That night when my mother arrived
at the precinct, David was already there. She'd called him and
told him what she knew, and he'd immediately found out where
I was and came to see how he could help.

"Hey, I'm here to inquire about my little brother, Yusef Salaam."

"Are you here in your official capacity?"

They knew him.

Linda Fairstein, the head of the sex crimes division; Elizabeth Lederer, the prosecutor; and everyone else involved knew who David was.

This young white man asking about this Black kid from Harlem wasn't a small thing. David was the assistant U.S. attorney for the Eastern District of New York. Before everything went down, I didn't know how powerful that position was or what it meant. I just knew that there was this guy, who happened to be white, who cared. David was a young man examining his privilege before that was a *thing*. He was doing the work to give back and lift up. I'd been exposed to the other side of life in many other ways. Uncle Frank and Aunt Denise had moved from our building to a large house in Middletown. I wasn't a charity case when it came to the exposure that David gave me. But the brotherly love we shared was certainly beautiful. He was such an integral part of my life before and after the case.

Before, we hung out together almost every weekend. We ate pizza together. He was the first person that I ever saw dabbing the oil off his slice. *Who does that?* I was from the hood. We ate all the pizza with the cheese falling off and burning the roof of your mouth. But here he was, mindful of his health, I suppose, dabbing the oil. And guess what I do to this day?

I dab the oil from my pizza.

In hindsight, I understand that it was never about the pizza or the oil. There's a more impactful reason why that particular memory sticks in my mind. There was a fatherly quality to our time together. And a son mimics his dad. Maybe I picked up some of that.

After, he was the one who reinforced to my mother, "You have to fight for your son." He went as far as to show her how to do it. He was responsible for telling her what she needed to know about in regard to the nuances of the law, and he gave her the information she would need to make the documentation. David, at the precinct, was able to make note of how much time had passed, who was doing what, and any other details my mother might have needed. For instance, he would say, "Hey, I'm here to see Yusef at nine o'clock." And they'd say, "Okay, we'll find a place for you to sit down and talk to him." But, of course, an hour or two would go by. He knew that there was something odd about that, so he was writing down who was who, so my mother would know whom to address and whom not to address.

My mother knew—as a parent, as someone who'd been in the fight for justice—to say to the detectives, "No, you don't have the right to talk to my son." But David Nocenti emphasized, "Do not fall back from that position. That is your position. That is your right." That was his character. In many ways, he was our secret weapon. He knew exactly what to give us so we could fight that fight in a powerful way.

David didn't have to play the father role. But he chose to.

He made a choice to leverage his privilege, get involved with the Big Brothers Big Sisters organization, and meet this kid named Yusef. He made a choice to stand by me. No matter how much trouble it made for him. And he still stands with me to this day.

Left to right: my brother, Shareef; my Big Brother, David Nocenti; and I after the premiere of *When They See Us* at the Apollo Theater.

FOUR

95A1113

The power of the white world is threatened whenever a black man refuses to accept the white world's definitions.

JAMES BALDWIN

Me in Central Park. This photo was taken the day before we were arrested.

THERE ARE WAYS IN WHICH we define ourselves and/or allow others to define us. Self-definition was literally the key to my overcoming what happened to me. The American justice system had painted an image of me as a predator. Holding on to my true identity, despite what was said or done, was how I survived in prison and how I have been able to thrive outside of it. And now people have rightly made assumptions about how well I'm doing since my release and the civic case and settlement. They see that I have a thriving career as a speaker, author, and consultant, and they want to know how any of that is possible in light of having years stolen from my formative early adulthood.

However, my understanding of myself was continually challenged internally and externally at every turn. There was the media characterizing us as wild beasts. There was my own sense of sorrow at not being able to articulate myself in all the ways I would have liked because I was a child. I faced numerous moments in which I had to refine my identity and hold fast to it in the face of grave danger.

Sometimes it was about establishing my worth and value

despite what the environment implied, in very simple ways. The day I was taken down to the local precinct in what amounted to a mass roundup of Black boys in Harlem was one of those moments when I had to grasp for what I knew deep down about myself. Raymond, Kevin, and Antron were already in the interrogation room. After Korey and I had our horrific turn, they locked us all up. Nothing really stood out about the cell I was in, other than the bars. I was still wearing the long trench coat I'd been arrested in. The Triple F.A.T. Goose coat was the height of New York hip hop fashion in the late '80s, and I loved that coat. It was black on black and complemented my six-foot frame. But I was so exhausted. Being shuttled to and from the courthouse and inundated with the flashing lights of the press, the finger-pointing and name-calling, was all taking a toll. Being that terrified is nearly indescribable. I felt panic rising in my chest whenever there was any movement. My eyelids were heavy with fatigue. Living alongside my fear was also relief. I wasn't in that interrogation room anymore. The walls weren't moving. I didn't have to suffer through listening to my friend Korey cry out in pain as they punched him.

I was also aware that the cell was not a place they likely cleaned very often. The dirt and filth sat thick on the floor. So, I took off that treasured Triple F.A.T. Goose trench coat and gently laid it across the ground. I stared at it for a moment, wondering if all the joy that filled me when I'd first gotten it really mattered in the big scheme of things.

I remember feeling so sorry that I had not listened to my

mother. She'd say to us all the time, "I came from the Jim Crow South," but I would brush it off. This was the 1980s. Times had changed, I thought. But I realized in that cell that I shouldn't have ever believed that somehow it was a different time.

They are about to do to me what they did to Emmett Till.

I was so sorry I didn't believe her. She was only trying to prepare me, teach me that this oppression was real. It didn't matter that I was innocent. I know the cool thing nowadays is to claim being "woke." Well, no one should be violently awakened in the way I'd been.

I knelt beside the coat and laid my weary body down to rest.

Well, at least I got my jacket.

It was such a simple act of defiance. Though I didn't recognize it as such at the time. But in hindsight, I see that the way I used my coat as a barrier between me and the dirt was a starting point of establishing my self-value above everything else.

I also see now that there was a kind of innocence in how I approached the questions I was being asked during interrogation. I knew who I was. I knew I didn't do what they were suggesting I did. So surely they'd figure that out, right? I struggle with remembering what the precinct looked like. I see the building only in flashes of memory. But I do recall the room being drab, a dark gray box. I could hear the clock ticking loudly on the wall. There was no light. No windows. It was so easy to lose track of time. Just like in casinos, where there are no windows to indicate the passing of day into night, the criminal justice system doesn't want you to know what time it is. How long you've been there. Time is a slug pulling you slowly away from your cognition.

But I do remember the interrogation:

I am in there going crazy. They bring me in and because they won't feed us until the next morning, I'm delirious with hunger. I'm thinking about the lamb chops I'd just put in the oven before heading out. *I told Shareef and Aisha I'd be right back.* The room is changing shapes. It feels like my mind is beginning to play tricks on me; their faces swarm me like angry bees. The detectives are monsters, a bunch of goons. Like angry gorillas at the zoo. And I've just fallen into their cage by mistake.

Every once in a while, they come in and question me. I tell them everything I know. They leave and come back again.

"When are you going to tell us about the lady?"

"What lady? What are you talking about?"

I'm racking my own brain trying to help them. *Help* them. This is who I was. Who I am. Someone who tries to help when there is a problem. To find a solution. I'm thinking, *I'm a good guy, so of course I'm going to help them out.* I don't know anything about Miranda rights, what it means that my Miranda rights have not been read. I don't know that they can and will use anything I say against me. I just want to help so this can be over. So the room can stop spinning and shape-shifting. So I can go home.

The next thing I know, I hear my friend Korey getting beaten up in the next room. Korey's not even a suspect. He's come to the precinct to support me.

༄

When I'd come home from school the day after going to the park, the courtyard outside of my building at Schomburg Plaza was strangely quiet. *Wow, I don't see any kids outside.* I wasn't immediately alarmed. It just was something that I'd noted. I went upstairs and changed out of my uniform. When I came back down with my street clothes on, I ran into Korey's girl-friend, Lisa. When she saw me, she said, "Yo, what happened in the park last night?"

"What do you mean?"

She ignored my question. "When you see Korey, both of y'all come up to my house."

"Okay, cool."

A little while later, I met up with Korey. "Yo, let's go up to Lisa's house." When we arrived, the news was on the television. Breaking news.

We were sitting there watching all the things they said had happened with wide eyes. But Lisa was watching us. Finally, she said, "So what's up?" We just stared at her blankly. We didn't know what she was talking about. She said, "They are saying it was y'all!"

"What?"

I asked, "Yo, Korey. Where'd you go last night? I didn't see you." I'd knocked on the window of the chicken spot he and Lisa were at to ask if he wanted to go to the park. We'd gone together but, frustrated, he'd disappeared early on.

He said, "Man, they started bugging. I was out of there."

I said, "Well, I didn't see anything like that happen in the park. I saw people getting harassed, and this homeless guy get beat up, but nothing like what the news was describing."

Lisa had said the cops were looking for us, so I simply reasoned that I'd talk to them to clear our names. I'd just go to the cops and tell them what I saw. I knew I didn't do anything. I didn't see anything. *I'm going to just get myself out of their hair and be home before my mom gets back.*

Korey and I left Lisa's, walked down toward Third Avenue, talked for a bit, and then walked home. Looking back, it's outrageous to think that I was actually looking for the cops to tell them my story. But this was 1989, New York City. This wasn't the Jim Crow South anymore, right? My mom was teaching that night at Parsons. I'd just put some lamb chops in the oven. My sister was making salmon for herself. Surely I'd be fine.

My brother caught wind of what was going on.

"No, you can't go!" Shareef had always been a little bit more muscular than me, even though he was a year and a half younger. He grabbed me and we started wrestling. "Don't go."

I couldn't get out of his grip. We were rumbling and banging into the walls. Korey was outside, but he was like, "They're brothers. I'm just going to let them do what they do."

Shareef continued tussling with me. When my sister said, "I'll go with him," he finally let me go. He turned to her. "You've got to promise me. You're going to go with him?"

"I promise."

In hindsight, it seemed prophetic. Like my brother sensed something he couldn't exactly articulate. We didn't always hang out together like I did with our sister. He had his own circle of friends, and I hung out with my sister because she was older and could hip me to what girls wanted.

Korey and I left with Aisha. When we exited the elevator, we saw cops getting in another elevator. I decided we should go back upstairs to talk with them.

One of us had to get up there first. So Aisha went up in a separate elevator just in case somebody pressed a button and delayed us. When we got up to our floor, the twenty-first, the police were standing in front of apartment 21 H, already at my door.

What I didn't know until much later, and my brother never told me, was that they were trying to get my brother to come down to the precinct with them. Shareef was not involved in any way, form, or fashion at all. He didn't hang out with us; he wasn't there at the park.

Any Black body would do.

They saw me as I came around the corner in my Triple F.A.T. Goose. "Hey, who are you?"

"I'm Yusef Salaam."

"Oh, that's one of the guys we've been looking for." They searched me, patted me down. "What's in your pocket?"

"I have a pocketknife."

It was a gemstone cut into the shape of a bird, with a little blade about two inches long, and very, very thin.

I also had my hospital medical card from Mount Sinai on me, which had all my information, including my correct birth-date, which they'd later claim to have not taken. And then there was the infamous bus pass. Back then, the passes were made out of paper and had a hologram on one part and a space to write your name and birthday. Instead of saying I was born in 1974, which was true, I wrote 1973.

Why?

For older girls, of course. To prove I was sixteen instead of fifteen. And that dumb-kid move would be what the police used to justify interrogating me without my parents present. The medical card would be conveniently lost.

They took us downstairs. As we came into the courtyard, I raised my hands.

"Put your hands down."

"Oh, okay."

Korey was still there with us. They turned to him and he gave them his name. He wasn't on their list.

He wasn't on their list.

But he agreed to go with me. To help me. In my mind, we were going to clear this all up and get home as fast as we could. Unfortunately, besides that brief time when I made bail, I wouldn't return home for nearly seven years. Korey wouldn't return for thirteen.

He came with me because, like he always said, "I got you."

Neither of us knew that Korey couldn't help me. That I couldn't help him. They separated us. They worked on both of us in tandem. He caught the brunt of it because he was sixteen. In the system's eyes, he was a man. But he wasn't. And neither was I. We were boys being steamrolled by the wheels of injustice. And they were attacking him. I think that was the moment, hearing Korey being assaulted, I knew that no amount of me trying to help them would change their minds. They were determined to frame us as criminals.

There were instances on this journey when I was not only determined to maintain my own self-definition but when divine grace afforded me the opportunity to do just that.

The three of us—Antron, Raymond, and I—were moved around quite a bit. We were the first to go to trial. Korey and Kevin would go later. From the local precincts, we were sent to a place called the Tombs. The name was definitely a metaphor for what the system did to the humans held there. The system wanted us to die.

What shocked me the most was the fact that there were grown men there. I was fifteen and there were forty- and fifty-year-old men in cells next to me. Men who'd definitely seen some things on the inside and out. Men who used violence often as a shield for pain they couldn't articulate. We weren't children to them. Some of those men would yell out to me: "Yo, big man!" And despite the terror filling every part of my body, I'd respond, "Hey, what's up?" Without batting an eye, they'd say, "Yeah, man. We're going to get you. Wait till we get our hands on you."

This wasn't some cool jailhouse banter. Rape wasn't the

charge you wanted on your head when you went to jail. These were folks being sent to Rikers. These were people who understood what I'd yet to understand about the predicament I was in. That the system had already targeted us and there was nothing left to do but to accept it was happening. I refused. All I could think was, *This is crazy. They're going to figure this out. They have to. This cannot be my life.* I was holding on to what I knew to be true. Despite the threats being yelled out to me from the next cell.

Because the Tombs was simply a holding place—many people called it purgatory—we were sent to Spofford Juvenile Detention Center in the dark of the following night. It was starkly quiet when we arrived. I could hear my own heart beating as the silence overwhelmed me. We'd been in holding up until that time. But we'd heard that while Spofford wasn't Rikers, it was nothing to play with. Like an eerie calm before the storm. Fear was playing double Dutch with my mind. Leaning in and out, seemingly waiting for the right moment to enter the jump.

There was a golden rule at Spofford that likely came in from the streets but took on an even greater meaning inside: "Don't sleep." Just like in the hood, you didn't want to relax too much. You didn't want to get too comfortable. You didn't want to feel too safe in any space or with any person. Sleep was the cousin of death. Because of who I was, who I knew myself to be, I didn't always follow this rule. I knew I didn't belong there to begin with. But one day, I paid the price for that defiance.

Due to the notoriety of the case, I was held in an isolated unit.

But one day, I got a chance to spend time in the dayroom. There were plenty of other inmates there, moving about. Unfamiliar with most of them at this point, I sat in the back and played the wall, meaning I made sure that I kept my back up against it so no one could creep up behind me. I kept my eyes open and with heightened awareness as I sat watching television. I sat attentive, making sure to periodically check my surroundings. After a while, though, I went from sitting straight up to sitting back a little. Something in my mind was telling me, *Everything's cool. You're good.* So then I relaxed. That chair became my grand-mama's chair in the way I let it cradle me. I got comfortable. Then, suddenly, I felt my face swing to the side. It didn't register that I'd been hit. In that exact moment it felt like I had an out-of-body experience where I was saved from the brutal force and pain of the impact. I was bleeding from a cut above my eye; my face started swelling, but I was simply...confused. *What just happened?* When I stood up, I saw that the officers had jumped on this massive man, named Guzman, who looked like the King-pin in *Daredevil.* They were wrestling him to the ground.

He'd hit me. Possibly with a weapon, although I could never confirm that. The cut over my eye was deep enough that it affects my peripheral vision even to this day. I still don't have full range of motion in my neck.

They put me and the other guy in isolation and later made us talk. I felt embarrassed. What would I possibly say to a man who'd caught me slipping like that? I didn't want to talk to someone who'd just tried to kill me. But the system wasn't concerned about my feelings. They needed to ensure I wouldn't retaliate. They wanted to avoid a lawsuit. They needed this assault to go away. But in the way that anxiety would surge through my body at times, it never really did.

That experience taught me to never "sleep," and I carry that with me to this day. I learned that no matter how comfortable you think you are, never get comfortable. You have to have eyes in the back of your head. That anxiety still showed up beyond prison, and even now sometimes, having reshaped itself as hypervigilance. In my early romantic relationships post-release, you'd never see me be lovey-dovey, holding hands, gazing into her eyes. I couldn't lose myself in that feeling. It didn't happen because I always needed to be on point. It—whatever my mind believed *it* was—could go down at any moment in time.

That experience also taught me that while I must maintain my own self-definition and never allow the system to tell me who I was, I couldn't ignore my environment. I couldn't sleep on the daily danger I faced while existing in that space, while being accused of a crime whose nature would ensure further assaults. And while I had to maintain my guard externally, I had to stay on guard internally. I had to regularly tell myself, remind myself, that I was not who they said I was. So I could live to tell the story.

I learned so much about the grace of Allah in that moment. That assault symbolized my whole experience of God's protection. In the same way that I somehow did not feel the full brunt and devastation of Guzman's hardened fist, I was blessed to not feel the full brunt and devastation of my time in prison, particularly in comparison to the experiences of my brothers in this journey. The Netflix series *When They See Us* captures their stories very well. I agonize over what Korey endured. As I watched the way each of us processed the pain of being accused of something so heinous, I'm clear-eyed about the fact that my experience in jail, despite the assault, despite the time spent in isolation, could have been so much worse.

∾

When I aged out of the juvenile system at twenty-one, I was moved to Clinton Correctional Facility. This is where I learned my biggest lessons about how hard the system works to make Black men and women believe the lies they make up about us.

Day in and day out, I would hear the heavy footsteps of the guards walking down the galley. They would yell, "On the gate. On the count." When you hear that, you have to get up, say your name, and say your number. Then you can go back to doing whatever it was you were doing. There's a repetition to it. The number is drilled into you. It's your identification, your brand. It got to the point where regurgitating that number became a knee-jerk reaction. Hear the gate. Get the call. Stand and say my name and number.

One day, while I was walking around the yard, a few of the old-timers came up to me.

"You Yusef?"

"Yeah."

The oldest of them said, "Come with us."

I was older now, but it didn't mean I wasn't still scared. *Man, I can't punk out now. Damn, I didn't survive all this time just to be killed in the yard.* I began thinking about my escape plan. Where was I going to run to? Most important, if I ran, would the guards even care? But I went. I didn't feel like I had a choice.

I followed them into the far corner of the football-field-sized yard. Or at least, that was how vast it felt to me in that moment. My mind was racing. *Man, they're going to kill me. They're going to kill me in the corner.* There was a man shadowboxing. I mean, this guy was killing the bag; every lick was a merciless demolition. I knew that if this man hit me, there was no question about it, I was going down. He would not only crush my face, he'd slice it wide open. *Damn.*

"We found him."

There was a pregnant pause and I'm pretty sure the whole world heard my heart beating. I was very tense. I didn't want to show fear because this was another kind of jungle and fear would only feed the ones who wanted to harm me. Like Notorious B.I.G. raps, "Your heartbeat sounds like Sasquatch feet. Thundering, shaking the concrete." That was how my heart felt.

My chest was puffed out, giving me an air of confidence that I didn't have. I readied my chin for a blow. The man took off his gloves and extended his hand. "As-Salaam-Alaikum." This means "May the Peace from the Owner of all Peace be unto you" in Arabic. His name was Adbul Haqq.

I let out a comforted sigh and said, "Wa-Alaikum-Salaam wa

Rahmatullahi wa Barakatuh," which means "and May the Peace and Mercy and Blessings from the Owner of all Peace be upon you as well." As Muslims you are taught that when you are greeted, you should reply with a greeting that is equal to it or better.

The man looked me in my eyes with a deep intensity. "We are Muslims. We are also members of the Black Panther Party and the Black Liberation Army. You are a political prisoner. You are safe."

At Clinton with Sheikh Albert "Nuh" Washington, an original member of the Black Panther Party and the Black Liberation Army. Men like Sheikh Nuh were the reason I was kept safe. Sheikh Nuh died in prison, never able to come home a free person.

Relief washed over me like a soft summer tide. I was twenty-one then, and I'm sure I didn't understand the depth of everything that was happening in that moment. I didn't know that they had been preparing for me. Waiting to find me. That they couldn't wait to meet me so they could make sure I stayed safe. I didn't know any of this, but I was so grateful. There I was, locked up in the mountains, fifteen miles from the Canadian border and being greeted by people telling me I am a political prisoner. They affirmed me in ways I didn't know I needed to be affirmed. I was not who the media said I was.

This helped exponentially in the formation of my identity, particularly as I approached release. It introduced me to a part of my culture that I had only read about. The Black Panthers. The African warriors of old. All the men and women across the Diaspora who fought on behalf of those whom the system had captured. It was the catalyst that would send me on a lifelong journey of studying Black movements for liberation.

Later in my time at Clinton, Luqman, one of those same elders, took me aside and gave me some additional wisdom. He was an older guy who'd been in a good while. An intelligent man who was always reading, and with so much wisdom behind his eyes. He came over to me one day and said, "Hey, young brother. You know what that number means?"

He was referencing the number I'd repeated so often that it felt embedded in me by that point.

95A1113

I said, "No."

Luqman, in the kufi cap, was very wise. These men were like my brothers. The gentleman on my right went to a bodega to get food for his family one night, was accused of a crime he didn't commit, and came home many, many years later. This photo was taken twelve years into his exorbitant prison sentence.

I didn't know. It was a significant part of how the state identified me and I had no idea what it meant.

"Check this out," he said. "Ninety-five is the year you got sent to the big house. The next part of your number is either *A*, *B*, or *R*. *A* is the whole first half of the year from January through June. *B* is the whole second half from July through December. *R* means that you returned after you left—that you got caught up in the door of recidivism. Your next part is your position in line. The number 1113 meant that you were the 1,113th person to enter the door."

I was the 1,113th to enter the doors of Clinton in 1995.

I was floored.

I thought, *You mean to tell me 1,112 people came into this facility before me, and my birthday is in February? That means from*

*January first to February twenty-seventh, 1,112 people had already
entered the system.*

There's a weight and magnitude to that. These were fathers.
And grandfathers. Cousins and brothers. Sons. When we ask,
"Where are the men?" here, in part, is the answer. I remember
turning to look at Luqman's number. It began with *72A*.

I felt sick.

I thought about all the prisons in New York, all the prisons
in America. This man had been in prison for longer than I had
been alive. He entered in 1972. And the *A* meant he'd never
gone home. I almost wished he'd had an *R*. That would have
meant that he'd have gone home at least once to hug his children or play dominoes with his friends. It would have meant
that he hadn't spent every waking moment since before I was
born behind bars.

The American criminal justice system is eager to define
Black men specifically, and Black people in general, as criminals. Mass incarceration is the corrupt system that allows those
numbers to actually mean something, to actually define a person. This system of injustice uses incarceration as a way to avoid
the problems of poverty, wealth gaps, and health disparities,
among many others, all wrought by white supremacy and the
history of enslavement and Jim Crow. Instead of uprooting the
system, they justify it, wielding incarceration as a social machete
to chop down the marginalized. It is the echo of states' rights.
It is the echo of a Confederacy that was desperate for a way
to continue the institution of slavery. It is the ownership of

humans by another name. Cornel West, in *Black Prophetic Fire*, emphasizes not only the fact of it, but the *why* of it:

> There are hundreds of political prisoners right now in America's jails who were so taken by Malcolm [X]'s spirit that they became warriors, and the powers that be understood them as warriors. They knew that a lot of these other middle-class [Black] leaders were not warriors; they were professionals; they were careerists. But these warriors had callings, and they have paid an incalculable and immeasurable price in those cells.

There's a plot that is more devastatingly powerful than we could ever imagine embedded in this system. As scholar and Afrocentric education advocate Jawanza Kunjufu has written about significantly, this plot is the conspiracy to destroy Black boys. He says, "Our youth are chameleons and they will become whatever we want them to become." The challenge we face is that the system has already decided who they want our youth to become. But it's up to us to decide differently. As Kunjufu also says, "We must demand excellence of ourselves and agitate and advocate justice from the larger society."

Mass incarceration is supported by other faulty systems. Housing discrimination and inadequate public-school education. Unemployment and lack of access to health care. Too many of us look around our communities and are utterly uninspired. We look around us and hear what the world is *really* saying: We aren't worth anything. Fortunately, there are many Black people who are countering that narrative. Many who are expanding what others of us see of ourselves. But that work isn't for the faint of heart.

Children go to Central Park and see the gentle streams of water and budding flowers. They play on equipment that's new and safe. Then they return to their neighborhoods and, from a psychosocial perspective, internalize the lack they see around them. They go to their playground with broken, hazardous equipment and they believe they don't matter, that they are not deserving. And sadly, for some who don't get to see a vision of themselves beyond their immediate environment, or who don't have the village of people to impart wisdom and knowledge of their true identities into their minds and hearts, they end up learning that the only place they can really thrive is the modern-day cotton field called prison. And so they return again and again.

I recognize that I was privileged in many ways throughout my experience in the system. I encountered so many people and opportunities that shielded me from the system's agenda. So much grace came my way. I know that too many people didn't have this same experience. But I also know that Black people have an extraordinary capacity for resilience. So, whether it's facing jail time for a crime we didn't commit or facing the grief of a lost job or loved one, we have the capacity to shift the narrative. We must be willing to define ourselves for ourselves. No, we may not have all the information we need. We may not have all the emotional and psychological resources at hand. But we can still be seekers. We can continuously work to discover new information about our circumstances. We don't have to buy the first story told to us about what's happening in our lives. We have the ability to sift through all the narratives and use that knowledge for our own good. We have to be willing to go on a journey. It's a scavenger hunt, for sure. So you must arm yourselves.

For anyone who is embarking on this journey, I suggest using the four *W*s and one *H*.

Figure out **who** and **what** you are.

Embrace **where** you are.

Search out **why** you are.

Learn **how** you are.

Keep digging. Keep searching. Don't accept the proverbial number you've been given. I was not *95A1113*. I am Yusef Idris Faadel Abdus Salaam. Even if, for a season, you have to repeat that number to *them*, as I did. Even if you need it to survive the moment. Know deep down that there is more to you, that grace will show up for you also. Just take the first step.

FIVE

Elevate and Decide in the Air

I have discovered in life that there are ways of getting almost anywhere you want to go, if you really want to go.

LANGSTON HUGHES

Early on in Harlem Valley, coolin' in the North.

To BELIEVE THAT SOMEONE IS guilty simply because they match the race of a perpetrator is a deeply rooted outgrowth of the white supremacy that's embedded in every major system in this country. As Aberjhani writes in his book of essays *Illuminated Corners*, "It becomes more and more difficult to avoid the idea of black men as subjects of not just racial profiling but of an insidious form of racial obliteration sanctioned by silence." The truth of that is profound. There are myriad ways to examine how law enforcement profiles and stereotypes Black men, but the one that truly reveals the insidiousness of the way the system operates is the spiritual perspective I take when I think about what happened to the Exonerated Five. And what continues to happen all around the country. The mechanism used to oppress marginalized people is most certainly a kind of witchcraft. This witchcraft has planted seeds of inferiority to the extent that too many Black and Brown people believe Black and Brown men and boys will be dead or in jail by the age of twenty-one.

I saw it myself while locked up. There were way too many men who were unable to stay mentally free and who succumbed to the defeatist nature of prison culture. There were men I encountered in prison who believed the lies they were told about themselves. But there were also those of us who literally fought for our freedom. We spent time doing whatever activity we could to launch our imaginations outside of the cinder blocks that threatened to choke out our souls.

My stabilizer of choice was poetry and art. For a season, though, it was also basketball. Prior to going to jail, I never really played basketball. Whenever I say this, people are shocked, since I've been over six feet tall since I was twelve years old. But even from a young age, I was an artist. Sports, with the exception of skateboarding and martial arts, just wasn't my thing. I spent many years studying jujitsu under Master Li'l John Davis, who was one of the top two instructors in New York. But there are no dojos in prison. And when I first arrived, I felt an overwhelming need to settle in, to try to connect with other inmates in any way possible as long as it was positive. I was still a child, and when I saw other children playing basketball, I wanted to fit in. *Oh, wow. That's cool. I want to do that.* Yes, I became a spiritual leader at Harlem Valley, but I was also a kid.

I'd been given some advice before going in, and now I kept hearing it over and over again in my head: *Do the time; don't let the time do you.* So basketball it was.

In Harlem Valley, my fellow inmates immediately believed my height would give me an advantage.

"Yo, Big U"—that was a nickname they had given me—

"you need to come on and get out here on this basketball court," they'd say.

So I began to learn the game. I started shooting and making more shots than I was missing. *Okay, this is cool.* I figured out what the other guys already knew: My height was an asset. And then I started dunking the ball. *This is real cool.* For the first time since the end of the case, I was actually enjoying myself.

The hours spent playing ball didn't make me feel like I was in prison. It was like I was back on the block with my friends again. Riding my skateboard. Telling big jokes and laughing big laughs. Having that taste of childhood gave us all back our humanity. Yes, we were in the belly of the beast, but there was still life there. There was life in this downtrodden space that we could turn into something beautiful, if only for an hour. So I kept learning and getting better at the game.

Some of these men were monsters on the court. It was like watching Michael Jordan play Scottie Pippin every day. Their talent was astronomical. I still may not be a sports person, but what I do love about it, and loved about basketball especially back then, is that no matter what team was playing, the sheer athleticism present on the court made you stand up in awe. That was how I felt watching people like Pamzy and Asiatic play in prison. These men were just as good, if not better, than the men who played for the NBA. The system just got them first.

Some of the most brilliant minds are sitting in a jail cell. The prison system houses some of the most amazing talent that will never be discovered. I watched guys who were ambidextrous

Pamzy, Kevin, and I during a visit. We all came from the same neighborhood.

and could maneuver in ways I still find astonishing. One guy in the adult facility, Lefty, was the type we'd let do whatever he wanted to do. He'd mastered every move we'd see the pros do in NBA games. He was doing crossovers and reverse layups like Jordan and Magic. Lefty was definitely not the guy you tried to post up.

There was Asiatic, who soared through the air so high, you could almost stand beneath him and see the bottoms of his shoes. He was another one who, if the scouts recruited from prison, would be a first-round pick. One day, he took an enormous leap, hitting his tooth on the regulation-sized rims we had on the court. From that point on, he was known as the man with the dead tooth—which was as much of a compliment as it was a dig.

Every day on the court was like a mini training camp. Because of that, whenever we were off the court, we were preparing for our return to it. In the cell, we meditated on moves. In the courtyard, we used weights to work on strengthening our legs. We were always thinking about what we'd just seen during a game we'd watched, or about a move our favorite player had made back in the day, trying to perfect our own. I discovered that in order to really live through your sentence in prison, it's important to find a way to document your time there, to find some kind of outlet. Basketball was that outlet for many of the men inside. There was this sense of "If I don't play, I'll get trapped here," and in more ways than the obvious. I don't know if they were always conscious of it, but they were using basketball to remain free.

In the youth facilities—Harlem Valley, in particular—there were so many guys who would do anything to avoid going to the adult prison. Including lying about their ages. I remember men just disappearing because the system finally figured out they were twenty-two instead of fifteen.

That happened to Asiatic. When we played ball, everyone wanted him on their team. Not just because he was good—like I said, many guys were good—but because his level of skill included elevating your own game. When I would play with him, he'd throw me the ball, and suddenly I was dunking the ball and doing 360s. Then, one day, he was just gone. Never returned to the court.

Apparently, he was older than he said he was. The fear of

going to adult prison was real. It's like somehow people knew that it would be much harder to find mental freedom there. In the youth facility, the older you were, the less likely you were to be assaulted. No one tried you. When you went to the adult facility, you knew you were going to be tried from the very beginning. You had to establish yourself quickly and ruthlessly or you'd be at risk of becoming a target. In the youth facility, you could definitely be confronted with a fight. That was common. But in the adult facility, a fight meant you could lose your life. In Harlem Valley, people would put soap in a sock and hit another person in the head. In Clinton, those socks could be replaced with tuna cans from the commissary.

This idea of being mentally free even when you are physically captive reminds me of an old Nike T-shirt I saw once. Underneath the trademark swoosh it said, "Just elevate and decide in the air." That was what we all learned to do. We found something that would allow us to elevate, even if only for an hour of our day. In that time, our ability to decide who we were was returned. In that elevation, we were liberated.

Elevating and deciding in the air is something I would use as a mantra once I returned home from prison. While attending Hunter College, I had many amazing professors. One in particular, Dr. Marimba Ani, taught us so much about Africa, including West African spirituality. She wrote:

Our cultural roots are the most ancient in the world. The spiritual concepts of our Ancestors gave birth to religious thought. African people believe in the oneness of the African family through sacred time, which unites the past, the present and the future. Our Ancestors live with us.

Dr. Ani added scholarship to our understanding of being the *kings and queens*, as we called ourselves in hip hop culture. She introduced us to people like Dr. Frances Cress Welsing, who reminded us that Africa was the starting place of mathematics and science. It was Africans who taught the world geometry and trigonometry. Our Eurocentric educational systems may have taught us to hold up the Greeks and Romans, but they only regurgitated what the Africans had taught them. My mind was blown on the one hand, and I felt affirmed on the other. Something in me knew this on some kind of cellular level already, but hearing it all confirmed through the books I read and the lectures I attended, after having spent time in prison for a crime I didn't commit—solidified the importance of defining myself for myself.

Smiling for my mom: She kept asking me to smile in photographs because I never liked smiling when having my photo taken.

So when I think about those brothers in jail, ballin' like Jordan and Magic, I consider them captive royalty. I witnessed greatness. And in my witnessing, I experienced a psychological respite. Their aerodynamic leaps reflected a kind of athletic trigonometry that could come only from the DNA of a people with galactic intelligence.

That said, there was another side to my experience with basketball. One that was less about elevation and freedom and more about some people's inclination toward envy. I didn't realize at the time I was learning and enjoying basketball that I was also in what they called "Gladiator School." In jailhouse ball, there were no rules. There was no such thing as "calling a foul." If you were hit, you were just hit. All that mental freedom and no rules meant that someone was going to get hurt.

It wasn't long before I became *that* guy. The one that other men would say, "Oh, we want Yusef on our team." I was new to the game, but I'd learned a few things from playing with these great players. I figured out that more than height, I had speed. I regularly thought, *Oh, I can bake 'em.* More than anything, I was enjoying myself. There's something satisfying about the journey toward mastery, and I was finding that basketball was something I could work on. What I didn't know was that there were others who were not as happy about my development. They were plotting.

He looks like he is having too much fun.

I don't like that dude.

The first time I was tripped on purpose. Of course, I was

still playing sleep—soaring in the freedom of the moment—so I wasn't even aware that it was intentional. They were fouling me hard and I was just thinking, *This is amazing.* The second time, they tripped me again and actually really tried to hurt me. I was supposed to fall on my face. I was supposed to go to the medic with a bloody nose, but I didn't. I rolled right out of the fall.

One of the guys, the one we were all scared of, stopped the whole game.

"Hold up! Hold up! What the hell? How did you do that?"

Still oblivious, I said, "What are you talking about?"

All I knew was, they got the ball from me, but I was still on the guy. Yes, I rolled out but, *Hey, this game is so cool.*

Because I'd studied martial arts for several years before the case, I knew how to fall. It was a life lesson our master jujitsu teacher taught us. In life you'll inevitably fall, but it's how you fall that will determine whether you live or not. So we were trained in various ways to break a fall. For me it was an instinctual response, but for them it was fantastic. It gave them a reason to respect me. *We just tried to really hurt this guy, and he's still in the game.*

I suppose that is a real-life example of the constant grace I've been blessed with, despite the tragic circumstance I found myself in. Unbeknownst to me, my life before the Central Park Five case had prepared me for what I would encounter afterward in every way. I was protected even when I felt like I wasn't. I feel like God was like, "Oh, word, you're going to try to trip him up? But you don't know what I gave him years ago in martial arts to enable him to get out of that." And so life's constant attempts at hurting me got thwarted every single time. There's a privilege in that, I know. But I think we all can look at the hard parts of our lives and realize that we survived because we really did have the tools. It might not have felt like it at the time. We might have even been as unaware, oblivious, or naive as I was on that court, but when we make it to the other side, there's a Sankofa moment: of looking back to see how far we've come, in order to move forward to something great.

But that doesn't mean life—or in my case, these other ballplayers—will stop trying to take us out.

My basketball star days ended when I went up to dunk a ball on that same court and another player, seemingly frustrated because they couldn't jump as high as I could, reached up and ripped my arm nearly out of my shoulder. The pain was beyond anything I'd felt before; my arm was literally hanging awkwardly out of the socket. I'm pretty sure I asked for my mama, it was that bad. And of course, this sidelined me from playing ball because they had to take me to the hospital. I was devastated and felt like someone had snatched away the little bit of freedom I had found.

Damn, I can't even do the one thing I was enjoying.

That was the first of four times my arm was pulled out of the socket. The rough play became so frequent that, at some point, I stopped bothering to even go to the hospital. I'd just pop my arm back in place, scream really loud, and keep it moving. Most of the time I did it not to avoid the hospital, but because I didn't want to be on time-out. In the youth facility, time-out meant that all your activities were restricted. You couldn't go to the gym. You couldn't even shoot a ball or you'd get written up.

I eventually returned to the court but, if I'm honest, it wasn't the same. I had to play basketball *awake* now. I still had fun, but because I had to attend to the motivations of the people around me, I couldn't escape as much. My freedom was limited by the people who didn't want me to elevate as much as I did.

This isn't unusual. It's the necessary evil that comes with being great. You'll find the thing that makes you feel free and excel in it, but there will always be people who see that and, because your ability amplifies their insecurity, will try to pull you down.

My time on the court dwindled, yes, but it also pointed me toward something that I'd always been good at but never really dived into: art. I'd sketched things here and there, but since I couldn't play on the basketball court the way I wanted, I determined that I would redirect my attention. I also began reading more about this faith I claimed but didn't know that much about. For instance, I didn't realize that there was a difference between the Nation of Islam, the Nation of Gods and Earths (Five Percent Nation), and Sunni Islam. I ultimately used the loss of basketball as a tool for freedom, and to become who I was supposed to be. To edify myself through my own talents and gifts. Art, poetry, and Islam became my primary modes of mental freedom, and these were things that no one could steal from me.

I recognize the privilege in being able to find mental freedom in a system dead set on killing you, at the very least on a spiritual level. That's truly the witchcraft nature of white supremacy. And there were so many people I met in prison who couldn't unravel themselves from that kind of sorcery. Even those singular moments of freedom on the court or in a book could not stop them from getting caught up in recidivism.

There's a friend of mine, who's in prison right now, who was also in prison when I was first there. He was in Spofford serving a bid for a notorious case when I first arrived. He was known as the .25-Caliber Kid, and even as a juvenile he was a hit man. He was truly about that life, as young people would say. He was such an interesting personality, and we connected because he identified as a Muslim. He wasn't necessarily practicing, but like me, he'd come from a family of Muslims and that was the faith tradition he'd always known. In many ways, that was my story until I began to read and study the faith of my father and truly take it on myself. I remember thinking, *Oh, you mean you can't just be Muslim because your family is? You actually have to at some point accept Islam?* I still have my Shahada letter, signed by my Imam, confirming my official acceptance of the faith. But this guy, Mack Moton, like many people, didn't think of being Muslim in those same terms. At the time, it was just part of the streets.

In late 2019, I spoke with Mack, just to check in with him. He's been in jail off and on since I was there in the early '90s. Now, mind you, he's come home a few times. When I was in

Spofford, he was released. Then he came back when I was in Harlem Valley, having been sentenced to fifty years, which was later appealed down to twenty-five.

There was one moment in particular, during our time in prison together, when it dawned on me that Mack's journey in the system would look very different from mine.

One day a riot broke out in the facility because, according to some, there was a young man named Hansel Muños who was being influenced by us Muslims.

Hansel had come to us saying, "Man, I want to be a real Muslim. I'm being harassed. I like the protection you all give."

Inmates had been robbing him. Any items he'd get from the commissary—soap, Little Debbies—would get stolen. So he accepted Islam because, more than anything, we took care of our own. Abdur Rashid always made sure that nothing went down.

One day we were all in my unit and a guy named Erskine, a tall guy who was known to be belligerent, started talking trash about the Islam we practiced. He was a five percenter, part of a religious movement called the Five Percent Nation, which started in Harlem and was influenced by some of the tenets of Islam. Erskine always stood in opposition to us. He'd say things like, "Oh, that's not Islam; *this* is Islam: I, Self, am Lord and Master." It was like a competition for him. This wasn't the case with all the men who were with the Five Percent Nation. Many were like, "Oh no, y'all Muslims are all right." I was even in jail with Capone and Noreaga from the hip hop duo of the same name, and they were cool. But for others, there was definitely some resistance and beef. Their stance: "Fuck y'all, let's fight." Erskine was that kind of guy.

Hansel, our newest convert, came to us saying that Erskine and others were harassing him. I said, "Okay, well, let me go talk to them." I went over to the men and said, "Look, we're Muslim. We're about peace. Let's not do this." I don't remember what exactly the response was, but it wasn't positive. Tensions rose, things escalated, but, at least on that day, we all walked away without coming to blows.

The facility often allowed religious leaders within the population to move about more freely than others. Abdur Rashid and I were allowed to go to different housing units to minister to other brothers. We went to Erskine's unit to try to come to some kind of agreement or truce. Rashid began first, saying to him, "Look, we're not trying to be about war. We're not about fighting nobody. You know what I'm saying? Islam is about peace. We are just trying to be peaceful."

I will never forget the way Erskine took his glasses off. It was like he was moving in slow motion. His words came flying out in a staccato beat. "I'm not trying to hear nothing y'all got to say." Now, Rashid, whose cousin is Floyd Mayweather, was mostly peaceful, but there was a clear reason why he was our head of security. He was nice with his hands and his anger was legendary. In that moment, Rashid's anger went from zero to 1,000. I saw it on his face. He'd slipped back into the streets. His body squared off, and he was about to rip this dude apart.

Rashid was the type of person who was always in control. Even his rage was controlled. But it was still rage, and the officers saw it, too. They jumped in: "Y'all got to go." Again, that time, nothing happened.

For prayer, one of the many Muslim officers who worked on Friday, our holy day, would pick us all up and take us to the room where we would either listen to a sermon, lead a sermon, or participate in or lead prayer. One of the younger Muslims, a comedian whose name I don't remember, was late coming to the prayer room. I truly believe that, spiritually, it happened for a reason. He was not really late; he was right on God's time. If he had been on time, he might not have heard what he did. We were sitting in our circle, a time where we'd have conversations about issues in our community and make sure everyone had what they needed. When he walked into the room, he said, "Yo, man, they are planning on jumping y'all when y'all go back to the unit." There was no confusion. The *they* was Erskine and his crew. As the leader, I said, "Okay, we're going to have Brother Abdur Rashid take over." So Abdur Rashid, who studied Islamic strategy and war while I focused on spirituality, gave us our marching orders.

We knocked on the door to the unit and they opened it. They shoved me to the ground and when I looked up, I saw Officer Chris Johnson's face transition from "Hey, what's up?" to "Oh my God!" in a split second. Fists flew. When I could finally stand, I went in and started grabbing people off of others. Somebody grabbed me and we fell on a couch. I was holding the person in place trying to keep him from swinging. But then I saw my friend Mack before he saw me. He reached over the couch ready to take out whoever was there. He had a razor in his hand, but I could see in his eyes that he was back out on the block and that razor was his gun.

He was mentally at war. I knew right then that it would be such a hard road for him to ever come back. Thank God he saw that it was me before he "pulled the trigger."

"Oh, y'all all right," he said, and kept fighting.

Finally, this tall West Indian guy named Bigga jumped up, put his fingers in the air, and said, "Peace, Muslims. No beef." By that time, though, no one was listening. I let my guy go and walked through the unit as everyone—officers and inmates—was still fighting and wrestling. Officer Chris Johnson was holding down a Muslim brother named Harmel. In hindsight, it reminds me of how police officers handle people on the streets today, holding the man from behind, his head turned over his shoulder. Harmel was moving as the officer's grip was tightening around his waist. The officer was yelling, "Stop resisting! Calm down!" What the officer didn't know was that another man, David, was behind him punching Harmel in the face. Harmel wasn't resisting. His body was responding to blows that the officer couldn't or didn't want to see. When I saw David advancing a third or fourth time, I could no longer sit and watch. I put my foot in his chest, Jim Kelly–style. David flew into the wall and slumped down.

Usually, when there was a melee in prison, especially if it was in the mess hall, they would automatically shut all the doors by lowering these iron gates. This happened later when I was in Clinton. When the gates lowered, you were even more trapped. Then all of a sudden, from the ceiling, pods of tear gas would drop and explode.

I wish that was the worst of it.

Next, the "turtles" would arrive. These were officers dressed in full riot gear. Everyone in the room would be laid out on the ground and, trust me, if you tried to get up, they would lay you back down—maybe even permanently.

Thank God that protocol was not used in this one instance at Harlem Valley. But when other officers came into the unit to help subdue those who were fighting, I said in a calm voice, channeling Spike Lee's version of Malcolm X to all the brothers, "Everybody line up."

We all lined up on one wall and prepared ourselves to be sent to what was essentially solitary confinement. There was no alternative. We were the ones who came in there, and despite the backstory, it looked like we were the aggressors.

When we finally returned to our different units, I ran into David, the guy I'd kicked in the chest. I was anxious and uncomfortable. *What would he say? Would there be continuous beef between us?* Tension hovered over us until one day he looked over at me and said, "Hey, what's going on, man?" He gave me a pound handshake. "Yo, man, that was crazy, right?" he continued. "Man, you kicked me so hard in my chest. All of the air went out of me. All I could do was sit there." He laughed and, stunned, so did I.

"Yeah, man, you can't be hitting one of my guys like that. You were punching him in the face. He couldn't even fight you back. It'd be different if he could fight you back."

Just like that, the tension was gone. There wasn't going to be a problem.

But the face that kept coming to my mind then and even now was Mack's. Him coming over to the couch, ready to kill. There was something markedly different about him than I'd seen in some others. A hopelessness. A despair. He was, by definition, a poster child for recidivism. He was in the trap and not because he wanted to be. It was the sole option presented to him by a community that internalized the systems of oppression that ultimately sought to demolish it. Prison as a way of life was given to him so young that he didn't know anything else. Mack and his own mother were a hit-man team. This transgenerational legacy of crime as the only way to deal with pain and trauma was all he knew. One of the Muslim officers who was mentoring me, who ironically was named Muhammad Ali, told me he spoke to Mack and was so happy he was Muslim. "You could see death in his eyes," he said. To some extent, the prison-industrial complex, the way this thing is set up, makes it hard to change. You can have all the spiritual transformations you want, but it's going to go only so far in a cage. At some point in time you may be faced with a situation, like Mack Moton, even like my friend Abdur Rashid, where something switches back to the modes of survival you were used to on the streets.

When we talked in 2019, Mack began sharing with me how he'd just come to realize that the system didn't want him to live free.

"Yo, man, I saw your movie. I see what's going on. They gave me all this time. They don't want me to come out of here. And you know what? I just realized they never even evaluated my mental makeup."

Here was a person, older and wiser, saying to himself, *Something isn't right. There were other options for me, as horrible as the things I've done were, besides a cage.*

I want to believe that, at some point, everybody is redeemable in this system. Even if you committed murder, you went to prison for, say, ten or fifteen years. It wasn't like you were never coming home. But when the system realized that they could counter the elevation and wealth-generation of Black and Brown folks, first by the infiltration of drugs and second by exploiting the loophole in the Thirteenth Amendment—while abolishing slavery in 1865, it allows for "involuntary servitude" as "punishment for crime whereof the party shall have been duly convicted"—and incarcerating us for profit, the decision made "in the air" was no longer ours to make. The system figured out that ripping our arms out of their sockets would keep us off the court, ensuring that we would never play the game of life well in this country again. The country found its new cotton fields, and the Mack Motons and Yusef Salaams of the world were ripe for labor.

That kind of power is definitely a kind of sorcery. It turns bright-eyed boys like Mack into criminals instead of providing the resources necessary for them to do the healing work needed to have a fighting chance at life. When I speak to high schools, no one raises their hand when I ask students, "How many of you PLAN to be dead or in jail by the time you're twenty-one?" Nobody plans for that kind of trauma. Nobody asks for death and destruction to be their path. And yet, deep in their guts, some of them believe that this narrative is inevitable. The brightness of their eyes turns dark and their pencils become guns.

You can't talk about someone like Mack Moton without talking about the systems that positioned him and his family for the lives they lived. You can't talk about crime without talking about poverty, health disparities, and redlining. You can't talk about the urine and excrement in the elevators of the projects (translation: concrete experiments) without talking about the lack of mental health and other social services. Just like everyone the system targets, Mack took the lemons of his life and tried to make lemonade. No doubt the levels of trauma he experienced affected his mental health. And instead of addressing those mental health challenges, the system decided that his life had no value. So someone like Mack doesn't get the help he needs and keeps self-medicating with violence and criminal activity.

There is a source to it all. It's Newton's third law of motion in real time. Crime is a set of reactions that people should be held accountable for. But if the only response to these reactions is a cage, then the actions that follow will never be ones that promote healing or rehabilitation. And that, sadly, is by design.

John Henrik Clarke explains why the American system of injustice makes such a concerted effort to criminalize Black people: "It is not uncommon for ignorant and corrupt men to falsely charge others with doing what they imagine that they themselves, in their narrow minds and experience, would have done under the circumstances of a given case."

This is why my social justice advocacy work post-release has been so important to me. The system has decided that it can predict the number of prisons to build by the time a population of students reaches the fourth or fifth grade. They are actually using educational statistics to build cages for mostly Black and Brown people. And so it's up to those who want to see a different America to step in and tell the truth. For me, I was fortunate to have prominent Black male leaders come to Harlem Valley and speak to us. I was still untainted enough by this system to take in what they were saying and build on it. When I first got to prison, I had many conversations with mentors who taught me that "words make people." I never forgot that. Language creates us. It shapes us. Our ability to communicate well with each other is the key to our liberation. It's the same reason why the captains of European slave ships combined the various ethnic groups they captured. If we can talk to each other, we can overthrow the ones who claim power. Somehow, I knew early on that if I could, I would use my words to help us heal. I was chosen to go through this awful, terroristic accusation in order for *America* to be put on trial. And maybe so I can stand in a prison like those elders and mentors did for me and encourage others.

I feel called, by virtue of my experiences as part of the Exonerated Five, to expose this mass deception, the witchcraft in our systems. We've approached our view of this country's systems in the same way we shop online. We see the thumbnail image of a product and believe it to be a representation of the content and quality. Then we're upset when we open the package and realize it's not what it was presented as being. America has purported itself as a beacon of diversity and progress, and yet we are nowhere near where we need to be in that regard. And though the civil rights leaders worked so hard and the movement accomplished so much, we have to be careful that we don't allow ourselves to be deceived into thinking there has been more change than there actually has been. As Malcolm X said in his famous "Ballot or the Bullet" speech, "How can you thank a man for giving you what's already yours? How then can you thank him for giving you only part of what's already yours? You haven't even made progress, if what's being given to you, you should have had already. That's not progress." Our humanity belongs to us. And it's not progress to get what was already ours in the first place.

I do not pat myself on the back because I was able to escape recidivism while many succumbed. I am where I am now because of who we are as a people. I firmly believe we have this ancestral strength available to all of us. As soon as we tap into it, unlock the truth of who we are, we'll all be able to break the generational curses and operate at another level. We'll all elevate. We'll all fly.

SIX

Love and War

The ends you serve that are selfish will take you no further than yourself but the ends you serve that are for all, in common, will take you into eternity.

MARCUS GARVEY

GROWING UP, WHENEVER I HEARD my mother talk about the police, she would say things like, "Don't talk to the cops. They're not your friends." She would say, "If they come, let them break the door down." In my young mind, I would think, *Really, Ma? I can just open the door. We don't have to let them break the door down. We can help them.*

But my mother knew something I didn't. At least, I didn't know it until it happened to me. My mother was my modern-day Harriet Tubman, trying to show me the way to freedom by changing my naive outlook on the world. I didn't believe her until it was too late.

When we were being interrogated, my mother arrived at the station with fire in her eyes. There was no time for sweet talk and comfort. There was no opportunity for "Hey, baby, how are you doing? Are they treating you well?" Her first words were "Stop talking to them." She had to give me proper instructions to save my life.

Her underlying sentiment was clear: "I love you, but we are at war."

She had to teach me how to stand my ground before I knew what standing your ground meant. My mother was the woman who played French-language albums on Saturday mornings and took us to the Museum of Modern Art. She was the one who emphasized the importance of education and made sure that she exposed us to a world outside of our uptown apartment building. It was intentional but never obvious. She never said, "Yusef, read this!" But instead she created an environment that allowed me to learn and discover things that some wouldn't have expected. I could have found anything from stories about African kingdoms to books on Grecian art on our shelves.

Me, my mom, and my cousin Mieasia. Mieasia and I share the same birthday.

But my mother would often say, "I was raised in the Jim Crow South." I think my siblings and I were supposed to know what that meant, but I'm not sure we did fully then. Her family was part of what is now known as the Great Migration, a movement of millions of Black people in the United States from the rural areas of the South to the Northeast, Midwest, and West between 1917 and 1970. She'd experienced two worlds that, below the surface, were really one.

While we might not have understood her meaning, we did know her stories. Of having to turn off the lights in the car on the last few miles home so that she and her family would not be confronted by the Ku Klux Klan. "That's Alabama," she'd say.

"But, Ma, we're in New York," I'd answer.

New York is different.

My mother was sent to the city as a teenager to make something of herself. Our family held the same hope as many Black families in the South: that the North would offer more opportunities for advancement, that there would be less terror and fewer lynchings. She ended up going to the world-renowned Fashion Institute of Technology. She became a designer and later taught at Parsons School of Design at the New School, one of the top universities for fashion.

But having that impressive career and education didn't shield her from what it meant to be a Black woman in America. She was trying to teach us this duality. She wanted us to learn whatever they were teaching us in school. But at home, we'd read Assata Shakur and Malcolm X. She helped us navigate the days when we were questioned about not saying the Pledge of Allegiance. She was very matter-of-fact in her responses to things. "We do not pledge allegiance to the flag. We respect the flag and we'll stand up, but don't put your hand over your heart or say anything because this flag does not pledge allegiance to you."

She never went into any great detail about her own experience. She'd simply share a story here and there and create an environment where information about who we were as Black people was readily available. She helped us move through the world the way she did: always moving forward while acutely aware of the dangers lurking around her. I suppose she hoped that at some point the why of all she was teaching us would click. That moment came when I was fifteen.

> No, I'm not an American. I'm one of the 22 million black people who are the victims of Americanism. One of the . . . victims of democracy, nothing but disguised hypocrisy. So I'm not standing here speaking to you as an American, or a patriot, or a flag-saluter, or a flag-waver—no, not I! I'm speaking as a victim of this American system . . . I don't see any American dream; I see an American nightmare!
>
> Malcolm X

When I was fifteen years old, my family and I woke up to the "American nightmare." All of us—even including my mother with all her Jim Crow experiences—were wanting the American dream. We wanted the ability to live, and we longed for the pursuit of happiness. The ideals of our Constitution were the ideals we held: that all men and women are created equal. But we learned in the most catastrophic way that this was never written with us in mind, and in many respects it still doesn't apply to us now.

It's still a war.

We are certainly trying to make it apply to us. The good folks who may just be the children of former slaves and the children of former slave owners are trying to make those words true for all and are doing so in the face of continued systemic racism and oppression, white supremacy, and white patriarchy. But freedom is far from a certainty. If anything, that was what my mother was trying to get at when I was young: Work toward liberation but be clear about the reality in which you're living. During the trial and while I was in prison, my mother never lost hope. She never stopped pushing. My mother always made it clear that this wasn't an experience I was having in isolation. She was also there, experiencing this with me. Her Alabama sensitivities were still present. She understood that what happened to the five of us was something that had happened to many over the course of American history. But, importantly, she was unwilling to conform to any notion that justified that experience.

✧

I can't write about the war if I'm not willing to write about the love. I've often stated that the Central Park jogger case was a love story between God and His people, and I recognize that for some that's a hard pill to swallow. The assumption is that I'm saying God caused these awful things to happen to me and my brothers.

But that's not what I'm saying at all.

God used these heinous injustices to reveal to us our own power and purpose. If I believe in both God's omniscience and the presence of free will, then I can reconcile that God knew I would be placed in the crosshairs of the system and, because of man's free will, He didn't stop it. But He did soften the blow. Not only that, God ordained that I would not only survive this experience, but I would also live fully in spite of it.

Part of the way I've been able to thrive in light of my story is through detachment. There are times when I speak about myself in the third person. "Yusef went through this," or "His story changed overnight." This allows me to disassociate from the emotions of the experience so that I'm not constantly triggering the trauma. To keep bringing up the pain would not be helpful—to myself or to those who are listening to me speak. At some point, I have to allow the deep wounds to scar over and eventually heal.

If I'm speaking from a healed place as opposed to a triggered one, then I can be part of the solution. To continuously sit in that trauma could mean being overwhelmed by the weight of what happened and unable to move forward. Instead of saying,

"Damn, I really went through that," now I get to ask, "How can we make sure it never happens again?" Because I think, more than anything, we need to get to the place of finding solutions.

This doesn't mean that I haven't had to live in that trauma and release the pain that exists there. Release is necessary before you can detach or seek solutions. This release happened during the screening of the Netflix series that told our story, *When They See Us*. Korey, Raymond, Kevin, and I (Antron could not attend the private screening due to the death of his dear mother) knew that we needed to experience the film privately, together, but we didn't realize just how much we needed to purge emotionally in the process.

I remember walking into the Netflix studios in Los Angeles and marveling at the space. The walls were large screens with images flicking between them. There were stations where you could get healthy food, water, juice, or snacks. People smiled and waved at us. They all knew who we were. Up until that point, we'd never actually been celebrated. We were just some regular boys turned men attached to this huge story. This was the first time we'd experienced that red-carpet treatment. People in that room not only knew who we were, but they were also happy to see us. That was a first. I think some of us wished this had been the reception we'd received when we were first exonerated. Now we'd finally gotten ahold of the American dream again, even though we knew the nightmare was still very real.

We felt so special. And the moment was beyond anything we could have ever imagined. We soaked it all in until it was finally time to meet some of the executives. We were brought into another room. Ava DuVernay, the director, was there. A round table was covered with an amazing bounty of food platters. "We're likely going to watch parts one and two," they said. There was no conversation about watching all four episodes. Just parts one and two.

We considered one another as brothers. As brothers, the four of us walked into a small theater with three long rows of seating. Ava was behind us. We placed ourselves in the room, none of us sitting right next to the others. Perhaps intuitively, we knew we needed the space.

When part one started playing, I didn't know what to expect. I remembered having previously sat down with the writers of the series for eight hours, and the liberating and energizing feeling of telling them my story. But I didn't know how it would all come together, how it would look.

The sound track—everything from Eric B. and Rakim, and Public Enemy, to Boogie Down Productions—took me right back to late 1980s New York City. I was most interested in seeing how these actors and actresses would portray us. And from the first few scenes, the film had our attention. We were engulfed in it. You could hear a pin drop. There was no sound in the room except what was coming from the screen.

Soon, there was a quiet sniffle. Following that, a sigh. Then, a muffled sob. Seeing ourselves portrayed on that screen was the purging we needed. Every actor nailed it. And because they got it so right, we relived our traumas in that room. But we were together and we were safe, and so those tears were held sacred by everyone there. And when I say we cried? Whew! We sobbed with abandon. It was painful in some places. But it was also a form of freedom. It released us. And it healed us in many ways.

I remember thinking at one point, *Wow, men do cry in the dark.* I can't speak for the others, but I had entered the room with a certain amount of machismo. I'd been sure: *Man, I'm not going to cry.* But I did. And it was okay, natural. Watching that first part of the series, I threw that machismo out the proverbial window and broke down. It felt so good.

At the end of part one, we hugged each other so tightly. We hugged Ava and thanked her. We'd had our Sankofa moment. We'd been transported into our past with an eye on our future. We had needed to sink deeply into our experience in order to move forward.

After a brief break, we were excited about watching part two. This time, when they asked, "Are you all ready?" we said, "Yes, definitely! Let's go!" Sure enough, we had the same experience the second time. We sobbed and sighed. Our hearts were full.

There was a dawning upon us then. That moment was the true realization of having survived this. We had survived—even though we weren't supposed to.

We all knew that based on the way the system is structured, even if we physically survived prison, we weren't supposed to survive socially. Our experience was designed to break us no

At the after-party of Oprah Winfrey's special for *When They See Us Now*.

matter what. We knew *that* as soon as we came home. We were walking around, hiding in plain sight, because we knew the depths of the hatred people had for us. We knew that our best bet was to disappear. But we didn't disappear. And then there we were, sitting in the Netflix studios, with our story on that huge screen. We were fully present and alive in every way that mattered.

There was another, longer break after part two. We were high-fiving one another and talking about shared memories. There was such a feeling of camaraderie and brotherhood in that space, this sense that we not only survived this awful thing but that we also survived it *together*. This was another moment when I believe God revealed His love to us.

We weren't supposed to watch parts three or four of the series, but during our break, we went to the studio's rooftop and looked out at the Los Angeles skyline. It was so incredibly beautiful. For miles and miles, we could see mountains and lights in every direction. God was smiling on us at that moment. Then Ava asked, "You want to watch the rest?" We chose to keep going.

We watched part three and were healed all over again. It portrayed our journey to freedom and how we struggled to get our lives back once we were released. We were so grateful that our story was captured in this beautiful way. After another break, we reentered the screening room. Korey had not yet returned. Ava grabbed my hand and told us, "This is Korey's part; this is the TV version." The room was tense, especially for me. I didn't know what to expect. I knew Korey had endured something terrible, having been imprisoned the longest, but I did not know the depths of his story.

Ava was very clear with us. We could not leave for a single minute during this part. It would be disrespectful, and it would dishonor what this man had endured. We didn't move. But we also thought that we'd cried enough. We'd been torn down and built back up three times already. So, surely, we were on the other side of the emotionality of this.

We weren't.

Korey returned and we began part four. If we were sobbing earlier, we were ugly-crying after watching part four. And we didn't care. The emotion spilling out of us was raw and unfiltered. When the credits rolled and the lights came up, Raymond was the first to speak. With tears in his eyes, he went over to Korey and pronounced, "You're a fucking LION!" He grabbed Korey and hugged him so tight.

I was still processing. I knew that Korey believed I was the cause of his being incarcerated. That if he hadn't gone down to support me at the precinct that night, his life would have been different. To see his journey on that screen shook me to my very core. He believed that I was the cause of his being there, and he didn't know that I believed him to be the cause of our freedom. Without Korey, without his seemingly chance meeting with Matias Reyes, the actual rapist, without him moving Reyes to confess to the crime, we could still be locked up. And if not physically bound, then certainly still convicted by society.

But I also had to acknowledge my role in Korey's pain. His truth was front and center in a way that we'd never talked about and I could not, would not, ignore it.

I couldn't get up fast enough. Raymond had beat me to him. I wanted to grab Korey first, but then I got my arms around him.

"Thank you. I love you, man. You're my brother."

I grabbed everybody. "Yo, man, I love you all!" To feel that love, in that way, was everything we needed.

We'd never talked about what we'd gone through before this. We'd sat down and shared our experiences for the 2012 Ken Burns documentary *The Central Park Five*, but it would take another seven years to get this kind of breakthrough. For *When They See Us*, we talked with movie people. Sometimes we talked to a camera. We'd even had another moment in Tribeca Studios prior to the Netflix release, where we all apologized to Korey and had an emotional, vulnerable moment. But I'm not sure we fully knew then what we were apologizing for. Now the series spoke for us, and it was powerful. In the Netflix private screening, we were able to look into one another's eyes. We were able to truly see one another.

꙰

You hear Black folks say all the time, "Oh, you got the right one this time!" It's a way of announcing to our enemies that they may have made a foolish choice to test us. Well, that's how I feel about the Exonerated Five. We were the five right ingredients to reveal to the world just how devious this system is and continues to be to Black people. As hard as it was, and as much pain as we endured, it could have only been us. God would use that pain, the attempts to take our lives, as the special spice to catapult us into the future.

Without a doubt, there have been plenty of Black men who went through what we did. Who'd walked this road before us. They walked so we could run. We run for them. For the 72As still behind bars. For the guilty and the not guilty.

I really hate that Antron missed the screening. Of course, we understood. But there was so much healing and love in that room that I wanted him to share in it. I'm not sure if he ever got to see that shift of going from most hated to most loved. Not in the way we did in that screening. He's been with us at other

This is the first time the Exonerated Five were on a stage together. We were at the SVA Theatre, being interviewed by the late Jim Dwyer of the *New York Times* after the first screening of the *Central Park Five* documentary.

amazing events, but in that moment we got to speak and feel freely in ways that we haven't since.

The beauty of this is that everybody is at different stages of their healing journey. And it's all okay. Korey, Kevin, and Raymond might be in one place. Antron might be in another. I am at a different place. It's all good. Because we are all constantly healing. That's the work. Every time we tell our story, it's like a therapy session. We get it out of us. We get a little bit better. We are able to move through life a little bit lighter. And that's how we should all aim to move through the hard times. One step at a time. All so we don't become ticking time bombs of grief.

Antron screened the film afterward, so I know he felt that release also. And we connected with him later. But after that moment of bonding, we all got to step out of that screening room with a different outlook on our experience. We truly became the Exonerated Five, eschewing the Central Park Five moniker forever. We know who we are now, and we show up differently. It's not just about the story. We now are part of the civil rights movement, the human rights era. We survived a lynching. We are still here.

❧

This case was a love story between God and us because we are still alive to tell the story, to live and breathe and love and heal. We could have died without the truth being known. Like Emmett Till. Like Mamie Till. They knew, but the world didn't know. The world hadn't yet heard Emmett's accuser say, "I made the whole story up." What does that say about the criminal justice system? It says the truth about it. That it is actually the criminal system of injustice.

One of my friends, Ronique Hawkins, showed me footage from the Emmett Till murder trial. We all know the story. They began deliberations. They came back an hour later with a verdict of "not guilty," despite all the evidence. But during a break, one of the jurors was questioned by a reporter.

"Hey, what took you so long? What was your process for deliberating? What led to you coming back with a not-guilty verdict?"

The juror responded: "We knew we were going to come back with a verdict of not guilty. We just wanted to take a soda pop break so that we could appear to be doing our job."

We live in two different Americas. We live in the America my mother was trying to teach me about when I was younger. The one that birthed the Jim Crow South. The one that taught us we needed the Harriets like her to teach us how to live in a war zone, to equip us to survive it. And then there's the aspirational America. The America we hope to one day become. The one we hope to be proud of one day.

Bernard Kerik, a former police officer and police commissioner in New York City, summarized this perfectly in his book *From Jailer to Jailed*:

> Don't promote yourself as a country of constitutionality and compassion if you honestly believe that putting

people in prison and treating them like animals is justified. Stop all the hype that we live in a free and democratic society. I used to ramble on about the same stuff. But now—are we really a country that believes in fairness and compassion? Are we really a country that treats people fairly?

∽

How do you survive as a Black person in this country? How do you maintain a positive outlook in the midst of such sorrow and trauma? For me, prayer has been paramount in my ability to remain mentally and spiritually free. I know that not everybody believes in God or prayer, but no matter your belief system, consider it as communion with a higher force, whatever that may be for you.

In addition, there's meditation. If prayer is speaking your heart and making your requests known, then meditation is being still long enough to listen for the answers. Meditation gives you the power to be able to move throughout your day as if your prayer has been fulfilled. I achieve stillness through my breath. Through understanding the power of energy and how to move it around to my benefit. But more on meditation later.

I've found it vital to have some way of documenting my experience. It could be journaling, drawing, doodling, or any other creative expression. It's not about being good or having natural ability or talent. It's about drawing those emotions from inside your body and out onto the page. After basketball, I spent so much time in my cell writing poetry and drawing. I attribute it to my ability to process my feelings on a daily basis. Poetry allowed me to participate in the war.

I wrote a poem titled "The Revolution Will Not Be Televised," borrowing the title from the great spoken-word record by Gil Scott-Heron. Writing that piece while behind bars helped me to remind myself of who I was.

I can remember when that statement made me sad inside
Too young to be in it
Now I couldn't even see it, Why?
why couldn't the revolution be televised?
The Last Poets'
Gil Scott Heron
As I grew up I began to see
They left theirs and I too wanted to leave a mark on
    History
A Man in half and I wanted to bask
in the task that set men free
But a revolution
The Revolution, is where I knew I had to be
The Revolution will not be televised
They don't want to display the victory of those "Lesser Men"
The Revolution will not be televised
Smile I know
Because I am the Revolution!

Sharing my new rhymes with my sister. She not only encouraged me, but she would also advise me on the phrasing and make suggestions.

That poem reminded me that I have to be my own answer, and that I am the revolution. There's no white liberator coming for me. I have to liberate myself. And in doing so, perhaps I can liberate others. There's a verse in Islam that says, "Allah will not change the condition of a people until they first change themselves." There's another hadith that says, "When you come to Allah walking, Allah comes to you running." God doesn't necessarily meet you at the beginning. He sees and recognizes that you have started, and the creative force rushes to aid you. Then, in desperate times, He carries you.

The beauty of this concept of love and war, or maybe it's better to say love *in* war, is that it teaches you to be in alignment with a creative force. And in doing so, your vision can become your reality. In doing so, you're putting yourself in a position to be used in a positive manner. Your biggest hardship teaches you to reach for something greater or higher than yourself. But you have to trust the journey. You have to let go. You have to pray even if you don't want to. Then you must act as if your prayers have been answered and meditate. Just put it out there. Cast down your bucket. And then you have to document it. That documentation may look different for you than it did for me. Documentation looked like poetry and art for me. Perhaps it will look like dancing or biking or yoga or writing flash fiction for you. Documentation allowed me to remain mentally free even though my body was in bondage. No matter the form, it will help you to do the same.

SEVEN

SALAAM BALONEY!

Sitting at the table doesn't make you a diner, unless you eat some of what's on that plate. Being here in America doesn't make you an American. Being born here in America doesn't make you an American.

MALCOLM X

I COULD SEE THE HATRED IN their eyes. I was a sixteen-year-old child, but somehow that was not who they saw. When I rose to speak, I saw them shrink. They were forced to hide behind their false notions of supremacy. My words would cause them to retreat even further. It was just a rap. A lyrical defense. A reclamation of my identity before they dared to sentence me. Borrowing from the books my mother encouraged me to read, from Malcolm X, a man I held in the highest esteem, I opened my statement with, "I'm not going to sit here at your table and watch you eat and call myself dinner. Sitting here at your table doesn't make me dinner, just like being here in America doesn't make me an American. Let us begin."

Just hours before, I didn't know what I was going to say. Antron, Raymond, and I had already endured a grueling trial leading to our conviction on August 18. We were now faced with the sentencing. Our convictions were upheld on September 11, 1990. The moment the verdicts came in, I felt like my life went into warp mode. The word *guilty* caused the whole room to erupt, and it caused my heart to burst. At least it felt that way.

As soon as the gavel kissed the wooden bench, we were taken away from everything we loved. We didn't have the opportunity to hold our loved ones. Everyone in the room was crying, some in victory, others in sorrow.

My mother wasn't even allowed to be in the room because she had already been told one too many times, "I'm going to need you to control yourself." And then, "Officers, remove her from the court." My mother was my fiercest protector, so to hear lies about her son was too much for her. She'd cry out in pain or anger. She'd say things like "These are all lies. You're lying against my son!" She might have seemed stoic and self-possessed in all those photos of her, but it was still her baby boy's life on the line, for something she knew he didn't do. She wasn't going to stand for that. The verdict was delivered to her secondhand. But my aunt was there in that courtroom. So was my sister. They wanted to hug me, but the officers grabbed me first. They handcuffed me and took me to the back.

Of course, there is a disparity between the way Black people who are convicted of a crime are treated post-sentencing and the way some white people are treated. After the sentencing, not only was I not allowed to hug my mother or my aunt or my sister, but I also wasn't given a date in the future to turn myself in. But haven't we seen that happen for others?

Perhaps a "Hey, listen, go to your vacation home, eat some of your favorite grilled chicken and risotto, and turn yourself in, say, in two weeks?"

Or a "Is two weeks good for you? Okay, well, let's say a

month. Don't go crazy now. You have to do your time. But go ahead and prepare yourself and your family."

I'm being only slightly sarcastic. In the Black and Brown communities, a delayed start to doing time is practically unheard of.

When we were brought into that holding room, Antron, Raymond, and I broke down. All the emotions we were holding fell from our eyes and mouths in heavy sobs. We knew right then that we were all we had. The three of us were the first to go to trial, before Korey or Kevin.

At one point, our attorneys came to us and said, "It doesn't look like we're going to win. We didn't tell you all this, but there was an offer on the table where you could have copped out to something of a lesser charge. We may want to revisit that now. What do you guys think?"

This was hard. The guys and I had just barely come together in a brotherhood. I didn't know Raymond before the charges and I knew *of* Antron only because he lived right up the block from me. He was another guy from the neighborhood. In fact, Raymond was really more of the glue when it came to keeping the doors of this burgeoning relationship open between us all. He was the one saying, "Hey, let me make sure this guy is good." Admittedly, I was more of the *I'm going to do this time and not let time do me* person.

I was an outsider because I was out on bail. I was going back and forth from home to court from, say, nine in the morning to five in the evening, like a job. And then I would go back home, take off my suit, and hang with my friends. But some of the others weren't as fortunate. I remember saying to them, "I'm never going to agree to something that I didn't do. You could give me the rest of my life in prison before I'd do that."

I still was very much an individual at that point. I didn't yet feel part of the group. I knew that we were all being railroaded but, no matter what, I wasn't willing to profess guilt for something I didn't do. We were the Central Park Seven and then Six, before we became the Central Park Five. They had rounded up seven guys. And while Steven Lopez copped out to a lesser charge, received just one to three years, and came home almost immediately, the rest of his life is forever changed because of his acceptance of the plea deal. At the same time, there was the hard reality that we were looking at some serious time. And for some, that was a devastating pill to swallow. We were kids, so making these decisions about the rest of our lives was something we should never have had to do. Still, my stance was this: "They can give me the rest of my life in prison. I'm not going to cop out to a crime I didn't commit."

If I'm honest, I didn't know what that really meant. Nothing in my experience had taught me what "the rest of my life in prison" would actually look and feel like. But I just knew that for me, there was a very clear line. If you did a crime, you cop out. You say, "Man, how can I get the least amount of time possible for this crime I did?" But if you didn't do the crime, you fight. You fight for as long as you have to. That was the principle that I brought into the situation.

༄

Now, when I think about the three of us in that room, huddled together, longing for the arms of our families and friends, I imagine us as a modern-day Shadrach, Meshach, and Abednego from the Bible. We were three boys in a fire, but our innocence meant we would never smell like smoke.

There's another Bible story I'm reminded of when I think about that moment. A story that feels incredibly resonant in its mirroring of my life. The bible's Joseph—Yusuf (ﷺ) in the Qur'an—was once falsely imprisoned for rape. Genesis 39:20b–23 (NIV) says:

> But while Joseph was there in the prison, the LORD was with him; he showed him kindness and granted him favor in the eyes of the prison warden. So the warden put Joseph in charge of all those held in the prison, and he was made responsible for all that was done there. The warden paid no attention to anything under Joseph's care, because the LORD was with Joseph and gave him success in whatever he did.

There was no way I could have known at the moment of sentencing just how much my story would align with Joseph's/ Yusuf's (ﷺ). But what I did understand deep down was that I needed to speak.

We were locked up immediately. I'd come to the courthouse

as a free man because we'd paid the bond. Post-verdict, I would not leave again. I had to wait months before the sentencing, and every day felt like purgatory. So when the officers came to pick us up for the sentencing hearing and brought us to our attorneys, I asked mine what I'm sure all of us were thinking.

"I heard we have to say something before the courts. What advice can you give?"

The attorneys were very much of a mind to "say whatever it is you want to say. Say what's on your heart." But we'd also heard others suggest, "Man, throw yourself at their mercy. Try to see the least amount of time possible."

That didn't sit right with me. All I could hear in my heart and mind was my mother's constant refrain: "I was born in the Jim Crow South." I could hear the voice of my grandmother: "You're a king. You're a master." They'd instilled in me a pride and resolve that would not allow me to beg for a freedom I rightly deserved. I chose a different route. I had a private moment with God and prayed: "Use me. Allow my words to be purified and put whatever I need to say in my mouth and in my head." And then it just flowed. Lyrics that told that courtroom exactly who I was: a kid who loved hip hop and his mother and Triple F.A.T. Goose coats. A kid who'd read enough to know that the train they'd run over him with should have long been banned from the tracks. A kid who was innocent.

Let us begin!
Stress, stress is the anger that is built up inside

SALAAM BALONEY!

Rage is the anger that is no longer built
Taken on a sucker, that soon you have killed
American freewill doesn't mean you can kill
And take another person's life
You live your life trife
I'm a skill builder
So on skills I do build
Creator given knowledge to this wise black man
Soon to enhance
My words across the land
I'm a smooth type of fellow
Cool, calm and mellow
I'm kind of laid back
But now I'm speaking so that you know
Got used
And abused
And even was put on the news
And on cue, they gave clues selling out like fools
Check it . . . who did what
And who did who in
You're put in a situation that you don't know what to do and
Some people go wildin'
We're not down with them
Who would have thought we'd have to lock in

I stand accused

Checking the scene from how the situation was,
Instead of getting facts the media made you blurred
Now the people don't know,
All they see is the media
They never hear the blamed
Cause they're constantly deceiving us
The D.A.'s wrong,
This is her master plan
This case is not a case
It's just a crafted sham
Yo!!!!
Instead of trying to get your name made,
It's reconstructing the crime that really pays.
Islam, la illaha illallah,
Born supreme over shaytan, but no man is Allah.
Yes, I'm a science dropper on the righteous path
So how the hell could I take a rapist path?
Think about that and then think about this,
All my friends it was me they dissed
They're dismissed.
Because I don't really need any friends like that,
Like . . .
When I really needed you, where were you at?
I'm not dissing them all
But the ones that I called
They went and dissed me,
like I was an inch small

SALAAM BALONEY!

Like a rat, a mouse, not even a man
Wrongly accused, like the knife's in my hand.
How does it look,
Me clocked now I'm shook
But like Matlock, soon the accused gets off the hook.
It's real when she remembers and says,
Damn!!! the cops did you in.

I stand accused

You people stop . . . the racial disperse
Aye yo! You seen that kid Benson? He's in a hearse.
And so we take it to the Benson Hurst fields,
Whites have bulletproof vests, and we've got no kind of
    shields
How does that look they killed a black man,
Being black, it's time to take a stand.
In our situation you saw our faces clear,
But not mine, not because of fear,
It's because the black race was disgraced
And for the Muslims, they must have felt shamed
But I'm not to blame with the words you bought,
The media took their words to paper
The ones the cops distorted
I told the cops truth like this, and then BOOM!

Man they smacked my man Korey Wise in the next room.
Now I know why the Rasta's can't stand de Babylon
They never help they just babble on.
I used to think the people and cops were cool…
But who protects us from you…?
I stand accused!

I imagined myself not unlike Kool G Rap in his music video for "Road to the Riches." I was flowing, going in just like he did. When I hit the last lines of "I used to think the people and cops were cool," I conjured another hip hop hero of mine, KRS-One. I was a fan of how he'd blast the listener with knowledge through profound lyricism and artistry, and so that last sentence was an ode to him. As I opened my mouth, my eyes were barely open. Courage and confidence had taken over. This was my debut as an artist. My mother had told me, "Make sure your words are clear." They needed to be. They needed to hear every word. Not just for me. Not just for Antron, Raymond, Korey, and Kevin. But for Yusef Hawkins, the sixteen-year-old Black kid who'd just been murdered by a white man in Bensonhurst, Brooklyn. In that moment, with my heart beating wildly, I felt a kind of liberation. I felt like, *If I have no words left to say ever, then I'd said them all today.* I had to get it all out and let the chips fall where they may.

I was told that the people in the courtroom were nodding their heads to the imaginary beat in the room. That's the draw of hip hop. If you're open to it, the rhythm will capture you. I didn't need a DJ or a soundman. There was music in the message, and there was a message in the music. The beat pulsed through my words. They could feel my heart. I was feeling energized. Our supporters were encouraged by my fight.

When I finished, Judge Thomas Galligan's face was apple red. He was beyond angry. And, of course, he would be. This was the man folks referenced when they called Rikers Island "Galligan's Island." He was notorious for going hard on Black men and being easily "persuaded" by DAs to turn a blind eye to the truth. Ayesha Grice, a former editor for *Essence* magazine and a surrogate mother of mine, said he trafficked in "legal lynchings." In our case, the prosecuting attorneys needed someone who would allow for the boundaries of the law to be overstepped. He was their guy. Galligan was handpicked to preside over our case because they knew he would guarantee the outcome they were looking for. And it's judges like Galligan that affirm our present-day need for defunding the police and criminal justice reform. Nevertheless, his fury at my "last words" wasn't a surprise to anyone. He banged his gavel. "Order in the court! Order in the court!"

I sat down with my head up and back straight. Though I doubt I had any conscious awareness of it, I think my spirit was determined right then that whatever sentence came forward, it would not break me.

The next day, my poem/rap song was covered in the *New York Post* with the headline "SALAAM BALONEY!"

That hurt.

I remember the reporter running up to the front. She asked me, "Can I take a picture of your rap song?" She said it in such a warm tone that I thought she meant well. I thought maybe this would be a moment when the portraits the media painted of us would be more honest. I was still sixteen. Still full of hope, despite what we'd already gone through. I was so deflated when I learned that, once again, I'd been tricked. It was embarrassing. Gratefully, there were people, mostly from our village, reaching out to us with comfort. They told us to "stay up!" To "keep up the good fight." They reminded us that everything was going to be all right. I can't speak for the other guys, but something deep in me knew that to be true. The truth would eventually be revealed.

∽

It's surprising to me when I think about it now, but at that time, while I knew that injustice existed, I honestly didn't think there were any other innocent people in prison other than us. Chalk it up to being sixteen, watching too many crime shows, or swallowing the false narratives provided by the system, but it never occurred to me that there were easily thousands of others like us, imprisoned for crimes they didn't commit. And then I started meeting them. And not just in the youth facility. All throughout my time in prison, I met men who were clearly innocent. With the evidence to back it up. But what they didn't have was the resources.

Either they didn't have the ability to defend themselves, or the price for doing so was too high. The Central Park jogger case wasn't some anomaly. My case represents the hundreds of thousands of cases just like it. People who felt they had to cop a plea. And then those who were forced to do so. And while Kalief Browder didn't cop out, look at what the system did to him. A Black youth from the Bronx who was imprisoned at Rikers for three years for allegedly stealing a backpack, without ever having gone to trial or been convicted of a crime, suffering the torture of solitary confinement for two years. Two years after his release he hanged himself in his parents' home. Look at what the terror of that system made him do to himself!

So yes, it is important for all of us to stand up for ourselves. To show up, resist, and speak up in the face of extreme adversity and detractors. But I will never pretend like that resistance doesn't come without a cost.

My innocence and naivete protected me in many ways. I can't imagine how much more of this trauma I would have internalized had I understood the nuances of everything that was happening. I genuinely thought we had a chance of winning. When that was not an option, I genuinely thought that I could handle what prison would throw my way. Hope held me together in ways I've only recently begun to unpack. I still had grace for people. My youth protected me.

The system capitalized on this, too. We are in a country that has chosen to traffic in Black bodies. It's the basis of capitalism. And I know that we all participate in capitalism in a myriad of ways, but there is a baseline evil that exists in our white-led systems that dehumanizes a group of people for greed and gain.

It's the same evil that says, "Let's take that skinny chicken over there, pump it with all kinds of deadly chemicals to make it bigger, and then sell it cheaply in Black and Brown communities." It's the same evil that produced government cheese and rice made from chemicals and plastic. It's the same evil that ensures there is limited to no health care access for people made sick by the food sold in their communities. The same evil that demands these people still bring their sick selves to jobs that pay them less than a living wage. The same evil that adultifies children like me and the rest of the Exonerated Five.

The Prison Policy Institutes wrote about the increasing mass incarceration in a study done in 2000. The study noted, "Beginning in the early 1990s, crime rates began to decline significantly around the nation. During this [same] period the number of state and federal prisoners rose substantially, from 789,610 to 1,252,830—a 59% increase in just seven years." To feed the system of mass incarceration that in the late '80s and early '90s was growing exponentially, we were framed as men despite being children. This adultification is not new and still goes on today. It's why the justification for Tamir Rice's murder was that this twelve-year-old kid playing with a toy gun in a park looked like a man with a gun. The goal is to steal our childhoods. The systemic oppression created by white supremacy and white male dominance *has* to alter us in order to justify its evil work. So Black boys become men and Black girls become women well before they are actually adults. This is very important to the psyche of evil. If you can get people to believe that a child is a full-grown person, then they will not see them as children or treat them as children, and are then willing to consider them as unredeemable. They will not be given the same opportunities, benefit of the doubt, or grace that one would give a child. The justice system has never been about telling people the truth. It's never been about our humanity. It's only been about the bottom line: "They need to be killed or put to work."

At Clinton, our brotherhood.

Donald Trump's rhetoric during our trial was as indicative of that mentality as his actions are now. He took out a full-page ad in the *New York Times* to tell the world that we should essentially be lynched. He hated us and wanted the world to follow suit. His headline: *"Bring Back the Death Penalty, Bring Back Our Police."* His sentiment allowed for the tsunami of vitriol spewed against us to continue and opened the door for media personalities like Pat Buchanan to go full racist. He wrote, "If . . . the eldest of that wolf pack were tried, convicted and hanged in Central Park by June 1; and the 13- and 14-year olds were stripped, horse-whipped and sent to prison, the park might soon be safe again for women." There isn't much distance between those words and those of Darren Wilson, the police officer who killed eighteen-year-old Michael Brown in Ferguson, Missouri: "[Brown] had the most aggressive face. That's the only way I can describe it, it looks like a demon, that's how angry he looked."

The framing of child as adult provides the out, the substantiation for the evil being done. And here's the real horror: When you mark a person, once you strip away their innocence for the public, you can never undo it. It doesn't matter that we were exonerated. The media didn't care as much about that—about our innocence, about the role they played—as they did about vilifying us and calling us "wild beasts." They took years of our childhood that we will never get back. And that will never be okay.

Sadly, internalized racism is real. Adultification does not only happen at the hands of white people. There is a collective adultification that's happened also. Too many Black people have been tricked into believing what these systems (and those who drive them) want us to believe. In all the experiments and surveys on implicit bias, particularly with law enforcement, you see that Black officers hold biases similar to their white colleagues'. Black people, maybe even out of some kind of survival mechanism, make their Black boys and girls into men and women before their time. That's also why, in some of the most violent instances of police brutality, we've seen Black and POC cops watching it all go down. They, too, have been taught that *this*—a face and body like mine—is what a criminal looks like.

There's a moment when one wakes up to the truth about America. In the era of being woke, there's something even more pressing, even more revelatory about awakening to the hard facts of how this country has treated Black, Indigenous, and other people of color. America purports itself to be a country built on hope, a promise. But to aspire for something better doesn't mean hiding from the truth. Hope doesn't mean hiding from today's reality. As James Baldwin expounded, "I love America more than any other country in this world, and, exactly for this reason, I insist on the right to criticize her perpetually." Hope means confronting the knowledge and feeling of "Wait, I could be a Breonna Taylor," or "My child could be the next Tamir Rice." As Malcolm X said, we are awakened to the American nightmare.

But it's in that moment—that confrontation of truth—where

we have to make a choice to stand up and be counted. In that courtroom, I chose to go against what was suggested. I wasn't going to plead for mercy. Even before that, when they told us to not go on the witness stand, I chose to go. Sure, I was misguided in that regard. The DA ripped me to shreds, twisting everything I said into lies that fit the narrative she was writing. I believed that I was wise enough to be on the stand. To tell my truth. I didn't realize how insidious these people were. She was laying out her story to prove to the jury that I was guilty, and I wasn't prepared to handle that interrogation. But I was not going to let her have the last word. I had to stand up for myself. In my own way. And not just for myself, but for my comrades in that battle, too. I suppose I could have remained calm. Did the pleading. I'm certainly not judging anyone who makes that choice. But I was a fighter.

Consider Ahmaud Arbery.

Taking a jog through a neighborhood, he was followed, chased, and murdered by white men who believed their rights superseded his. Video footage shows Ahmaud trying to hold on to his life. With labored breath but still running away from the imminent danger. His humanity was being siphoned away with every slur in that confrontation. How could he not do anything but struggle? We see some police officers saying to people in these recorded accounts, "Stop resisting!" What we often don't see is that prior to "resisting," there is a back-and-forth between the officer and the person whose rights are clearly being trampled upon. That fight? That struggle? There comes a point, and I feel we are nearing that place now especially with the protests of summer 2020, when Black people will say, "Enough is enough! I will stand on the truth of my innocence, on the truth of our collective innocence, and if that means we lose our lives in the process, so be it."

A coward dies a hundred times, but a hero dies only once.

In some ways, standing in front of that courtroom and saying my piece was the only way I knew to fight back. My mother wasn't allowed to be there. My father was not there. I had to fend for myself. I had to save myself, and the act of trying to do so felt like something close to deliverance. By the grace of God, there is a hedge of protection that's placed around many of us for a reason. But then when we are ready, when we are faced with our reason to fight, all the things we'll ever need to show up for ourselves are there, inside of us, waiting to be used, waiting to help us. We can't focus too far ahead, though. We can't focus on the destination. We should focus on the journey itself. The process. So let us use our sorrow when it shows up. Let us use that anger when we feel it in our bodies.

As Dr. Maya Angelou tells us: We dance it. We march it. We vote it. We do everything about it. We talk it. We never stop talking it.

EIGHT

The Safest Man You Could Ever Meet

Umuntu Ngamuntu Ngabantu. A person is a person because of people. I be you, you be me, we be we.

ZULU PROVERB

O N THAT AWFUL DAY IN the police precinct, when I was being interrogated about a crime that I had no idea had happened, my eyes were still wide with hope. But my mother said something to me that day I have never forgotten. She said, "They need you to participate in whatever it is that they're trying to do here. Do not participate. Refuse."

She was right.

My very survival in the system was contingent on my never engaging or participating in anything designed to dehumanize or define me negatively.

"They need you. They need you to engage in this."

My mother was telling me that these detectives and prosecutors needed me to be complicit in whatever it was they were trying to do to us. If I complied, if I let them run me over, then I was in cahoots with the system, and that would be the real problem.

Don't be in cahoots, Yusef.

Because I entered the system at fifteen, there was so much I didn't know about building and maintaining relationships. As a teenager, you are at the cusp of your understanding when it comes to relational dynamics. You are moving from whatever engagement you have with your parents and caregivers to learning how to navigate friendships. For me, everything was amplified. Imagine being framed as a rapist, imprisoned during the critical years of your late adolescence, but in actuality having had only one sexual experience. Upon my release at twenty-three, I had to learn what it meant to engage in healthy relationships with people, especially women.

I'm still learning. Ask my wife.

One of my first lessons? The power and necessity of vulnerability. Black men have had all sides of ourselves worked over by society in general, and specifically in the media's representations of us. There are the stereotypes and tropes that have been carefully crafted for us: the criminal, the sexual predator, the Magical Negro, the Uncle Tom. That we are whole human beings with desires and yearnings for love is presented as unattainable or unrealistic. For the longest time, I understood romance and affection only as something that happened over *there* and with *those* people. I would watch a movie or read a book and see a couple holding hands, staring at each other on a moonlit pier. I'd think, *Oh, that's cool.* But I couldn't truly connect to those feelings. The trauma I endured at such a young age created a block in my ability to access the appropriate feelings for healthy relationships. It was hard to tap into those emotions.

I'd learned something different where I'd been. In prison culture, letting your guard down meant being taken advantage of—at best. When you come home, you have to constantly remind yourself that you aren't in prison anymore. Being free feels unnatural. *You mean I can kick my feet up and enjoy the sun in Jamaica? You mean I get to run around the park with my daughter, throwing a ball or pushing her on the swings? That doesn't feel right. Surely someone is coming to steal this peace away from me.*

Showing any form of vulnerability means death for too many of us. A Black man brought to tears because of the humiliation he experienced at the hands of a police officer is quietly seen as weak. A Black man who is hardened by these lived experiences of racist profiling and resists that humiliation risks his life. Ironically, not showing any vulnerability—being too strong, too hard—can also mean death. And if not physically, certainly psychologically or spiritually. We can't win. We aren't allowed to feel safe enough or free enough to reveal ourselves fully. This affects our wholeness, how well we are able to engage in intimate partnerships. We're half-empty glasses hoping to one day be filled. Without knowing what that fullness feels like. The notion of being awash with joy and love and peace without any strings attached seems wonderful, but completely foreign.

At sixteen, with hormones doing what they do to teenage boys, I had to find ways to keep myself together while locked up. To keep myself from unraveling. Islam helped me with that tremendously.

It's natural to long for companionship. For sexual intimacy. My body was afire. I thought about my girlfriend often. The touch of her skin. The sweetness of her kisses. My one sexual experience prior to going to jail, though not with my girlfriend at the time, played like a Memorex in my brain. What it meant to hold a woman, to feel her, was never too far away from my dreams. And yet it wasn't helpful for me to dwell on these things. If I did, it could tear me up.

I didn't want to be like some of the guys I encountered while inside. The ones who would look under the TV when watching music videos to see if they could "see" under the dancers' dresses. There was something about being institutionalized to that extent that made the natural unnatural. These men were simply trying to imagine something real but, as a young person, using my imagination this way wasn't what I wanted.

The Qur'an teaches restraint as a practice. It says that everyone should be married. If one cannot marry, then we should fast because fasting kills sexual desire. Prison gave me the opportunity to deep-dive into this aspect of my spirituality in a way I'm certain wouldn't have happened outside of that environment.

So, no matter the sexual feelings that would naturally well up in me, I had the space and time to practice the teachings that would hold me down. I could wake up for late-night prayers. I could read more. I could do all of this because I knew that when I woke up in the morning, I didn't have anywhere to go. I'd still be here. I could find some value in the lack of distractions. There was *The Cosby Show* or skateboarding waiting on the other side of the night to steal an hour or three from me. I had time to do the spiritual work, to put myself in a position to grow in my faith and ultimately become the teacher (Imam) for the Muslim community while inside. Hormones raging or not,

I was given a window through which to think about things differently. I could go deep and far and wide in my dreams. This version of mental freedom, where I could explore the heavens and plunge the depths of man's own philosophies, was the silver lining, what I call the beautiful side of prison. I learned early on how to be isolated and restricted yet simultaneously free. I also learned that sexual power is sacred and can be used to propel you into deeper and more profound truths. By harnessing the sexual energy that bubbled up in me, I was able to move and invest that energy in both intellectual and spiritual pursuits. The ability to abstain is the ability to transform your current reality.

I suspect there was also a part of me that didn't want to mess up. I didn't want to violate the tenets of my faith. Also, at any time, any moment, sleeping or not, someone could come by and do a room check. They would turn your cell over looking for contraband items. You couldn't anticipate when it was going to happen, and you never had an opportunity to hide your stuff. I'd gotten caught with a *Playboy* magazine and it didn't feel good. I remember being so embarrassed because a Muslim brother was the officer who caught me. When the brother pulled the magazine out, I felt the shame rising in my body. I felt like I'd let my teachers, my role models, and Allah down. He said, "Come on, Brother, you don't need this." Though in my mind, I was like, *Umm. Yes, I do.*

His correction was significant because it was my Muslim brothers who had protected me. After the first few months of my sentence, I no longer had any fear of being sexually assaulted by another inmate. I had groups on the inside who looked out for me, such as members of the Black Liberation Army at Clinton. But I also had our growing Muslim community, both at Harlem Valley and then at Clinton, ensuring that I wouldn't be violated in that way. This was how the Muslim community worked in prison: We protected our brothers and taught them the ways of Islam, but we also addressed their immediate needs, like a lack of money in the commissary or issues with officers. We were respected by officers who, when they observed someone truly practicing the faith, such as by attending prayer or studying, considered them a nonthreat and often gave them small freedoms within the context of the unit. When I became the Imam at Harlem Valley, I was able to extend those same protections afforded me to the other young Muslims there. I'm so grateful for their shield and for the opportunity to have *been* a shield, especially as I know that's not always the case for many.

I knew enough about my body and its needs to be somewhat aware of what was going on with it, even if I did choose to repress those urges because of my faith. Before the Central Park jogger case, I'd gotten my sex education from my aunt Denise. When I was a kid, she lived in the same building as we did, only seven floors up. Aunt Denise was our Diana Ross. Elegant and beautiful, she was the definition of a free Black woman. Educated, she was a nurse manager at Metropolitan Hospital. The same hospital that allowed the Central Park jogger, Trisha Meili, to receive the lifesaving care needed for her survival until she was transferred from Metropolitan to a medical facility upstate after her attack. The world is so incredibly small.

My aunt, my uncle, and my cousin Frank were all core parts of my village. Frank and I were like brothers, always hanging out. I'd yell out to my mom, "I'm going to Auntie's house," and there'd be no resistance. As such, my aunt, most likely with Mom's prompting, took it upon herself to talk to us about sex, including giving us bananas so we could practice putting on condoms. It was embarrassing as a teen, but as a twenty-three-year-old being released from prison after so many years, I was immensely grateful.

Part of the reason why I believe my mother called on Aunt Denise to talk about sex to us was because I'd gotten busted with a girl in our home. I wish I could say my first sexual experience was with my girlfriend, Asia. After I was arrested and made bail, I returned home for a moment. I met this young lady, and things escalated.

We were on our way to court when she walked past me the first time. She was my age, maybe sixteen or seventeen at the most. When I passed, she said something to me in Spanish. My first thought was, *Oh, that's weird*, because I thought she was Black. I didn't know anything about the identity of Afro-Latinos at the time.

Not speaking Spanish, I asked, "What was that?"

I don't remember what she said but I was intrigued. I later learned that she was living in the Bronx, and she'd found out my address. Not too long after our initial meeting, she told me that she planned to meet me and found out where I lived. She got a job across the street from where I lived to make it happen. Every day, she'd simply observe me, and though I was dating Asia at the time, with my fifteen-year-old hormones raging, I couldn't help but be flattered. I could tell that this girl was open to things that Asia, who was the classic "good girl," was not. The most Asia and I did was kiss and feel each other in the dark. We were teenagers doing what teenagers do. Testing boundaries. That is, until the criminal injustice system swoops in and destroys all that.

One day, things were getting hot and steamy with this girl, and she straight up tells me, "I'm going to give you some."

"Okay."

Of course it was fast. And wonderful. And a rush like I'd never experienced. A rush that was amplified by the fact that my mother came home while this girl was still in my room.

I had on a T-shirt and my underwear. My mom looked at me and said, "Who's in here with you?" I had to talk quickly. "Mom, it's my um, well, my um, girlfriend."

My mother said, "Uh-uh, she's got to go. Now!"

I was just a kid. I didn't understand yet what it meant for my mom to catch me fooling around with a girl in her house. I did try to explain myself, though. I said, "Ma, we were just in here chillin'." I was trying to sound as believable as possible—which was probably not working, since I was standing there in my underwear.

"She's got to GO!"

"Okay, I'm going," the girl said. She got herself ready.

I pleaded with my mother, "Ma, can I at least walk her to the elevator?"

Mom said, "You can walk to the elevator, but that's it."

Then I said, "Well, downstairs?"

"Downstairs."

Then I decided to push. "Let me walk her to the train station, Ma."

"That's it!"

So I walked her to the station, all right. But not the one near my building. I walked her from my building on Fifth Avenue four avenues over to the 4/5/6 line to get on the train and go back to the Bronx. When I came home, I made sure to tiptoe in. I knew I'd taken far longer than expected.

My mother was standing there in the kitchen looking at me.

"You want some ice cream?" she asked.

"Sure."

"Okay, go down to the store right now and get us some Häagen-Dazs."

Häagen-Dazs was my favorite. We never spoke about what happened again.

As you can guess, this girl I'd lost my virginity to turned out to be a stalker, who showed up pretty much everywhere, even after my release seven years later. I remember a more recent time, not too long after the settlement, when she reached out to me and asked, "But what about my money?"

Coupled with my release from prison, I carried the added stigma of being convicted of rape. The public nature of our trial and sentencing made meeting women somewhat challenging. There were times I was recognized, and it soon became evident that I had no chance with a woman I was interested in. There were other times when the realization would come later, and the woman wouldn't want to deal with me any further. There were also other uncomfortable and awkward encounters.

Most days, I just crept through life hoping that nobody figured out who I was. I met one woman in Mart 125 in Harlem. She walked in and made sure I saw her. I definitely did. I thought she was fly, but I had no game. I was still nervous about approaching anyone so, while captivated, I didn't say anything, and she left. A few minutes later, a man came up to me and said, "Hey, there's this young lady outside waiting for you. She said she saw you, but she didn't know how to say hi."

Whaaat?!

I went outside, and we talked a little and ended up in a bowling alley down on Forty-Second Street. After hanging out, I was excited. I wanted to connect with her, and we exchanged numbers and began talking. We'd have long conversations on the phone and then started dating regularly. She became my girlfriend. One day, while hanging out at her apartment, I decided to tell her my story.

"Hey, I have to tell you something."

I imagine this made her nervous. Anytime someone opens up with "We have to talk" or "I have to tell you something," it's usually not good. I didn't know what she'd do or say, but I couldn't let it fester for much longer. I knew I needed people in my life who believed me. Who would say, like some of my friends, "Yo, wow. Yeah, I knew you didn't do that. Don't even worry about that. You're my people." It was those kinds of affirmations that taught me who to keep in my life and who to let go. When I told her, her response knocked me over.

"You raped that woman, didn't you?" She smirked at me as if she'd found out a secret.

No, she couldn't have said that.

It was such a deep disappointment. I kept thinking, *I can't keep this person in my life. She is the enemy. This person is part of the enemy.* I tried to tell her the truth, but she seemed convinced I was something that I was not. The worst part was knowing that she would have been okay with me actually having done it.

Needless to say, I faded into the background after that conversation. Maybe the kids nowadays would call it ghosting.

෴

All these challenges with relationships likely fueled my reluctance to be vulnerable with people. I knew how to be charismatic. I knew how to be engaging. But being my whole self, revealing my sensitive side in particular, was difficult. I was always waiting for the proverbial room check, I guess, for someone to hurt me when they caught me with my guard down.

This was true even in my friendships. When I came home,

it took time to feel a semblance of normal. It took awhile just to be able to say, "Hey, what's up?" to people in the neighborhood without fear. I didn't think anyone would run up to me and punch me, or at least I hoped not. But it was a visceral feeling of exclusion. Of never being accepted. Of being treated with skepticism. We weren't exonerated yet. And while our small community overwhelmingly supported us, there were those in the wider world who believed that we were the monsters we were painted to be. I was afraid that I'd learn just how much I was hated, and it would shatter me.

Of course, there are people you just vibe more with in life. Pam and Shaharazade are probably my oldest friends since I came home from prison. We were all going to Hunter College

Some of my Hunter Crew: Shaharazade, Jacqueline, and Pam.

at the same time. They were the first to crack open the hardened exterior of my heart, to break down the walls I'd erected in fear.

There was a group of us who'd hang out all the time. We'd go out to eat and laugh about all the stuff going on at school. One of our favorite places was Dallas BBQ, on the East Side near campus. It was always a good time. Plus, it was 1999 in New York City and I was an artist and poet, so of course we'd all hang out at the spoken-word open mics held at Hunter. They made me feel more at home. In community.

One evening, about a month after I met them, we were headed to TGI Friday's in the Bronx. I pulled Pam and Shaharazade aside. "Hey, I've got to tell you both something."

Their faces were blank and expectant in the way that people get when they aren't expecting anything unusual.

"We're friends. But I don't want to continue our friendship without letting y'all know this."

I was terrified in that moment. We were all cool. No one in our crew knew who I was. As much as the press followed our trials and convictions, there was no wave of media when we were released. Some people knew what we looked like, but not everyone remembered. I was so scared about what they would say. I was racked with fear, wondering, *Will they shun me?*

"I'm Yusef from the Central Park jogger case."

Their faces changed. But they softened.

"Man, that was messed up!" Pam said. She grabbed me and held me so hard. "Welcome home, Brother."

It felt like a thirst had been quenched. As if my whole being had been refreshed in that very moment. I mattered to these people. I needed that support. We all need it. We all need someone willing to crack open the walls around our hearts. They showed me such care; their love and support poured into me, filling up the gaping void that I always felt inside of me. There's something about being believed. About being seen. They saw me and loved me.

Shaharazade and my first daughter, Rain.

Romantic relationships were more challenging, however. Hit or miss. Many women were like "Nah, Brother. You need to get that jail/probation together. You need to figure that thing out."

Some people expected me to wild out when I returned home. But that's a bit of a stereotype, I think. There are young people who think it's cool to go to prison, as some kind of rite of passage into manhood. Like a hood bar mitzvah. That misguided perspective is reinforced when they come home. And though people celebrate you because they have missed you, there can also be this twisted elevation. "You're a man now," they say. *All the ladies want me*, you think.

But that didn't happen for me. Because of the spiritual journey I was on, I was clear that I wanted to be married. I wasn't the type to hang out at the club. My brother would take me every now and then, and I would stand in one spot, panicking and thinking, *Yo, people are too close to me.* I had never been much of a club person anyway. I rarely went to the teen basement parties that people in the neighborhood would throw when I was younger. But post-release, clubbing was especially not a good time for me. I didn't feel safe. I'd play the wall just like I would in the facility. I'd have much rather been getting a bootleg DVD and binge-watching some movies.

One reason why, I think, marriage felt like something important for me to do was that I wanted to maintain my integrity as someone who practiced Islam. I didn't always fight my urges. I had multiple long-term relationships—including my first marriage, which did not end well. The demise of that relationship is not solely my story to tell. But part of the problem in that relationship was due to my inability to support my family in the way I understood a man and father should.

My record chased me, as it does so many of the formerly incarcerated. I firmly believe that the system is designed to disallow men who have been imprisoned to fully return to the roles of husband and father in a way that is valued—in terms of becoming the financial and emotional foundation of a family.

I wanted to take on the traditional provider role, and so I always questioned how, psychosocially, I was to find my place as a father and husband when the system had tried to strip me of my worth. I eventually got there, but it took a lot of time and pain.

LaKiesha and I met when she was nineteen and I was twenty-seven. She'd grown up very independent, having lost her mother as a child. When we first met, she said something to me that I understood the weight of only after our marriage fell apart: "I've been my man for so long. You have to teach me how to let you be my man." At the time, I brushed it off. Of course I'd show her. But I was still unraveling what being a man meant to me, and I had no idea what her vision or her expectations of me as her partner were. We met when she was a supervisor at Internet Customer Service Enterprise, on Forty-Second Street. I'd worked as a representative before being promoted to assistant supervisor. The training for this new role wasn't comprehensive—my boss said, "Learn from her," and so LaKiesha taught me what I needed to know.

We got married when LaKiesha turned twenty and quickly began building our life together. But we faced huge obstacles. I was only five years post-release. I was still emotionally and mentally extricating myself from the institutionalization I'd experienced. I was educating myself but trying to find my way in a world that still thought of me as one of those beasts in the park.

I don't think she really understood what it meant to be married to someone with a conviction like mine. It meant being fired from jobs; it meant that pain and emotional strife would show up in ways that restricted my ability to be vulnerable. I'd been pushed to the margins by the system. Because of this record, I was not fully restored to society, and so I was pushed out into the margins even further. Some men check out entirely. Some learn to numb themselves. Others, like me, find it incredibly difficult to connect emotionally and to articulate what we need in a vulnerable way. It hurt to be constantly seen as a failure. I couldn't mold myself into what we both understood about manhood—that a man must provide for and protect his wife and children—and it eventually destroyed our marriage.

But we still tried. We moved to Georgia for a stint. Packed up all our stuff and just left New York for a fresh start. We lived in the back room of a strip mall's storefront, where my friend from prison, Abdur Rashid, ran a production studio.

Our picture of what our lives would be in the South was very different from the reality we faced when we arrived. We thought maybe we'd get an apartment, a nice car. We did eventually get those things and slowly began to rise up out of our predicament. We moved to the Stone Mountain area. We had cars now and a decent place to live. But I still didn't have a job. She was working, but my record barred me from every opportunity I might have gotten. By then, the strain of living so precariously and being unable to reach each other emotionally had already broken what was barely hanging on in our relationship.

We had two children by the time we left Georgia to return

to New York City. We lived with my mother in Schomburg Plaza for a while until we found our "penthouse" apartment on 138th Street. Trust, it was a penthouse only because it was on the top floor of a six-story walk-up with no elevator. We had our third child shortly after moving in.

I knew things were really done when one day we'd stopped at the Barnes and Noble on West Eighty-Sixth Street. I couldn't find parking, so I pulled our Jeep Cherokee next to a fire hydrant to quickly run into the store. When I returned, there was an expensive parking ticket on the windshield. LaKiesha was in the car. I was confused.

Rain and me.

"Why didn't you move the car?"

She didn't have much of a response. She sat and watched the officer write the ticket and did nothing. She was done. In hindsight, I understand that I needed more validation from her. And I had failed her. We'd been married for five years but only together for two and a half, separated the remaining time.

When I told my mother we were divorcing, she consoled me. "Someone will love you again," she said. I wasn't so sure.

Even after that marriage ended, I struggled financially and emotionally. There was still this fear of being vulnerable. I explored a few other romantic relationships, but they never amounted to much. I didn't want to go there again without being prepared. Without, at the very least, being financially ready to support my family. I also didn't want another failed marriage. And honestly, no one I met was rushing to the altar.

Deep down, I knew it was going to take an exceptionally strong woman to deal with the baggage I was carrying. Thanks to Magic Johnson, I finally met her.

∽

I felt wrecked for years after the end of my first marriage. I felt like I was just blowing in the wind. I didn't have control over my life in the ways I wanted, and it messed with me mentally and emotionally.

One day, I found myself in my mother's office. I was working for her at the time, trying to make some extra money to help support my three children. I remember having an unusually strong urge to move, to take the trash out. I started walking around the office, emptying all the wastepaper baskets into a bag to then put in the alley for pickup. There was something going on in my head and heart. It was a spiritual prompting to move and keep moving, that only with the distance of many years I can see for what it was. Once I was outside, I felt my spirit moved again. To take a walk. In that moment, I just went with it.

I was on 138th and Frederick Douglass Boulevard, and I headed downtown. I didn't have a plan. I had no destination in mind. I just kept walking. The birds were chirping and the sun was hitting my skin in that tingly way, warming me from the inside out. At 125th Street, a still, small voice whispered again: "Go to Starbucks."

Now, mind you, I used to work there, regularly opening up this Magic Johnson–owned Starbucks on the corner of 125th and Malcolm X. I don't know why I was drawn to go in—I didn't have some overwhelming craving for coffee; I had no real reason to want to go inside, especially given my familiarity. I was just supposed to be there.

I entered the cafe and immediately I saw her. *Wow, who is this?*

There was something about her. She stood out, like a rare treasure. She was more than the typical around-the-way girl. Of course, I didn't know how to approach her, had no idea what to say. Thankfully, she spoke to me.

"Can you believe this? They ain't got no more soy milk. This gentrification stuff in Harlem is all crazy and I come in here, and they don't got no soy milk."

But I wasn't even hearing what she was saying because I was so mesmerized. I said, "Are you a model?"

I laugh when Sanovia tells this story because she swears that I "hit her with a line." It wasn't a line for me, though. I was enchanted by her. She was so stunning, I truly thought she was a model. I didn't know anything about modeling. I certainly didn't know that models are supposed to be tall.

"What? I'm five-two!"

We got our drinks and started walking down 125th, chatting. She was moving so fast, I at first thought maybe she was trying to get away from me.

"Hey, just hold up. Why are you walking so fast?"

She smiled, continuing to talk to me but never slowing her pace. She was walking like a New Yorker. And it had started to drizzle. A Black woman walking in the rain was bound to move quickly. And I was determined to keep up with her.

Talking to her felt like a welcome rainshower on parched and dry grass. It was nourishing; I wanted to soak it up as much as I possibly could. At one point, I even said, "Man, this is such a great conversation. I would love to continue it."

She smiled, surprising me with her response: "No. I don't give out my phone number."

I was not going to give up that easy. "Well, can I have your email address?"

"Okay."

And that was the beginning. I didn't know it at the time, but her initial hesitation had little to do with me. She was going through a bad breakup and was being very cautious. She wasn't interested in jumping into something immediately after the trauma of her previous marriage. But we did email each other quite a bit. I like to think that's how our courtship began.

Sanovia lived pretty close to me, and in the week after our Starbucks run-in, we started meeting at the train station. We both took the train downtown—she worked on Thirty-Fourth Street and I was working at the Weill Cornell campus of New York Presbyterian Hospital. Normally, I'd get off several stops before her to catch a bus across town, but this day I thought, *You know what? I'm going to drop her off at work.* I walked her to the door of her office and headed back uptown to get to mine. That simple change to my routine unveiled all of me to her. She told me afterward that a coworker had seen us and asked, "Do you know who that is?"

"It's just some guy who likes me."

"Do you know his name?"

"Yeah, he said his name is Yusef Salaam."

"Google him and come back to my office."

I was trying to take it slow with Sanovia. Baby steps. Something about how we related to each other felt right, so I wanted her to heal, while knowing that I needed space and healing as well. I'd had every intention of telling her my story. It was 2007, so I was less afraid at that point. The media storm had blown by, and I had been home long enough to say, "You know what? Take it or leave it." Even at her first hesitation to give me her number, I half-jokingly said, "I'm probably the safest guy you could meet." But I was also careful with the timing because I really didn't want to mess this up. I didn't want to know if she'd respond like the others. I was a few years out of a difficult marriage, and I didn't want any of that to influence what was blooming between us.

Of course, she looked me up online. And called me from work.

My heart raced as I considered the possibility of rejection. Rejection never came.

She simply said, "Wow. Tell me about it."

And I did. I let her ask her questions, which she had every right to ask, and I answered every single one. I was so grateful, and surprised, by her approach. She was inquisitive, wanted to know more. The opening in my heart, cracked ajar by my friends all those years ago, was now wide open. And after she heard all that I had to say, she responded in the most amazing way possible:

"Cool."

We started meeting for lunch occasionally. There were days when I noticed how tired she was; all that she was going through with her separation was taking an emotional toll. For me, well, I was just glad to be near her. Some days we'd hang out and she'd fall asleep. That small voice in my head prodded me toward compassion. I let her sleep. *I got you*, I thought. I was there with her, and that was all that mattered. That she was comfortable enough with me to do this meant everything. For the first time in my life, I knew without a doubt that I made someone feel safe.

It was the opposite of what I'd been told about myself for years. I was accused of something that would rightly make any woman feel in danger. So this simple act of her falling asleep in my presence opened something up in me on a spiritual level. It was part of my healing. Despite all the graces I'd known in my life, I still wrestled with the hole made by the trauma of my experiences. I was constantly battling this tension of knowing I came from greatness—defining myself—as feelings of unworthiness tried to seep in from the outside. I ultimately learned that self-definition had to happen outside of the prison walls also. In fact, I needed it even more as I was trying to acclimate back into the world. So when Sanovia fell asleep on my shoulder, I didn't fully realize the depth and significance of what was happening. I didn't know that someone else could be a salve and create peace in your soul until I found love again. Sanovia loved me back to life.

We've now been together for thirteen years.

Healing is such a shape-shifting thing. It happens in stages. The intimate relationships I've had were all part of the process. The relationship with my wife gave me the impetus to begin unpacking my trauma via storytelling. She believed in me, and her belief helped me to know I was okay. I'd certainly shared my story on stages since my release, but they were one-off, niche opportunities. I'll never forget the day I woke up, sat up in the

Sanovia and me.

bed, and said, "I don't want to go to work no more." Her faith in me was so absolute that she simply responded, "Well, don't go to work." Then she asked, "What do you want to do?"

"I think I want to pursue this motivational speaking thing full-time."

Her response: "Well, let's do it. Let's figure it out."

That changed everything on the inside of me. It drove me. She listened to my heart and responded accordingly. This opened the door to every opportunity I've experienced since then.

There will never be a moment when you say, "Okay, fine, that was good. I'm finished. All healed." No, tomorrow you might need to talk about it again, to heal a little more. Be okay with the time it takes. There's no need to rush it. What's for you is for you.

That early conversation with my soon-to-be wife about being unjustly convicted opened up that process for me. I learned that my story has value. That I can inspire people who are also doing everything in their power to not participate in the false narrative they've been given. It took awhile to go from saying "Thank God I survived that" to "I'm part of something greater. I'm a part of the civil and human rights movements." But it was the support I'd received that ignited that shift.

Find yourself someone—several someones, if possible—who sees you. Whether it's a mother telling you to not participate in your own destruction, a spouse who stands with you in the fight, friends who accept you with their arms always open, having a solid, supportive village of truth-tellers and nurturers makes all the difference in the world.

In Georgia (from right to left): Me, our family friend John Beckett; my mom; John's daughter, Kara; and our children in the middle. In the middle row, far left, is Korey's mom, Dolores Wise, and next to her, in the sunglasses and hat, is Sanovia.

NINE

The Expendability of a People

They have had to believe for many years, and for innumerable reasons, that black men are inferior to white men. Many of them, indeed, know better, but, as you will discover, people find it very difficult to act on what they know.

JAMES BALDWIN

Hopeful for tomorrow, and looking toward the future.

D UE DILIGENCE IS A PRIVILEGE afforded to only a few. During the trial and immediately afterward, the media took up where the justice system left off. They treated us in a way that told the world we were expendable. They didn't fact-check. They spewed whatever lies would drive the next day's story, and people believed them. Some of this narrative-building began during the trial, when our words were distorted. The law, in my experience, is rarely about the truth. It's about who tells the best story. And in the case of race, the truth sounds inconceivable in the minds of people who haven't experienced oppression because of the color of their skin.

I was on the witness stand and the prosecutor, Elizabeth Lederer, asked, "Why did you go to the park?"

I replied, "Well, I thought it was going to be fun. I always go to the park."

This shouldn't have been considered surprising or odd. Many studies have shown that access to green space in metro areas is reflective of broader class and racial divides. Due to limited access to parks and other green space in our neighborhood—a direct correlation to the white supremacy inherent in urban planning—the park made for a natural hangout spot for us. So the *truth* was that Black kids from uptown enjoyed hanging out with our friends at the park. But *that* truth was unbelievable to those who chose an alternative story: Any group of Black boys hanging out anywhere must be up to no good. So while I was thinking, *Of course they understand that teenagers can chill at the park without getting into trouble*, they were framing my recreation as nefarious and playing into existing stereotypes.

I imagine that the DA, having heard me say that I went to the park to have fun, thought to herself, *I got him*. When she asked her follow-up question, I still had no idea that I was trapped.

"Well, was it fun?"

"No."

And then she asked, "Well, did you have a basketball?"

At that point, I was baffled. *What does having a basketball have to do with me being at the park?*

"Did you have gym shoes or sneakers on? Why would you think this is going to be fun?" she continued.

I was terribly confused. Wasn't it clear? Because Central Park was our backyard. It was where we went to hang out. Where we went to experience nature and green space that wasn't available to us in our neighborhoods. To experience normalcy.

But this is nonsensical to those creating the story.

Black boys didn't go to Central Park to just hang out. And if they did, they'd have on sneakers and shorts, not Timberland boots. (Clearly, she'd never been to a street game in a Black neighborhood.) They'd certainly have a basketball, because don't all Black boys play basketball?

When I finally figured out what she was trying to do, it was like an epiphany, and I was so frustrated with myself. They were most definitely playing chess, and I wasn't even playing checkers. There was a complete imbalance of knowledge and experience, not to mention power.

They'd already predetermined the outcome. And when I say *they*, I don't mean just Lederer or anyone else in that courthouse. I'm talking about the systems of white supremacy and white male dominance. Oppression is the tangible expression of that. That's what oppression really looks like. There are people who believe that being a person of color means that you are automatically guilty, and the onus is on you to have enough receipts to prove yourself innocent.

While nowadays we have more opportunities to put the truth on blast, and we can use platforms like social media as tools to make our case, what we're still doing is appealing to America to see our humanity. We are still jumping through hoops to get crumbs from a table filled with bread. We're still having to say, "Hold up! Look at this videotape." The facts don't matter. The words and testimonies don't matter. We have to have this inordinate amount of proof for things that white people do with impunity.

Rayshard Brooks drank too much and fell asleep in the drive-through of a Wendy's. In his inebriated state, Rayshard questioned the police officers who awakened him. I can imagine him thinking, *I don't want to go against the law, but I also don't want to lose my life.* The police could easily have walked him right across the street to his house. To his mama's house. To his grandma's house. They could have said, "Look, you are not fit to be out right now. We're going to walk you home. Matter of fact, we're going to call an ambulance for you, all right?" They could have *not* said, "Breathe into this breathalyzer." But instead, those officers chose to handcuff him. I can imagine Rayshard's fear. I can imagine him wanting to get away. The narrative about him could have been that this guy needs help, and right now we'll get him to bed.

That would have aligned with the same compassion shown Dylann Roof, a man who shot up a church in Charleston and killed nine innocent people. After being taken into custody, he was brought Burger King for dinner because even domestic terrorists need to eat.

So even with more resources, we are still trying to prove our humanity by appealing to people who don't see us as truly human. We keep hoping that the system is fair. It is not. And it will be judged for that. There are too many people who have built their lives on the backs of Black bodies. And there will be a reckoning, spiritual or otherwise, for that.

Right now, there are people who are sitting in a jail cell and have not been arraigned. They have not been called up to be judged for whatever it is they have been accused of. What do they have except hope? There's a verse in the Qur'an that says, "On the Day of Resurrection he will be of those arraigned?"

(28:61). Well, I know what that's like. I know what finally getting my chance to tell my story before the judge means. But I also see this as an indictment for those who are enactors and enablers of the systems of injustice in this country. They, too, will stand before the judge one day. Until then, we must figure out ways to conquer these inequities in this earthly realm without continually having to prove our inherent worth as human beings.

This challenge is why I believe that many of us have decided on an all-or-nothing approach to justice. There is no "right way" to protest. Because the oppressors have determined there are no right ways. They have told us how and what they will accept, and yet even peaceful protesters can be met with tear gas. Marches and yelling are labeled as riots. Even taking a knee during the national anthem is enough to destroy a career. They mind us organizing. They mind us quieting ourselves and realizing the depths of what's at stake. They mind us arming ourselves in line with the very Second Amendment they try to keep for themselves.

Perhaps ancestors like Margaret Garner got it right. Garner was an enslaved African who was both vilified and lionized for killing her daughter rather than have her returned to slavery. The acclaimed writer Toni Morrison based the story of Sethe on Garner in *Beloved*. Underlying the horror of such acts is the same principle that many Americans celebrate in the founding fathers: *Give me liberty or give me death*. There is no more capitulation to a system that doesn't care. Our humanity keeps us hoping, and that does good for our souls. But the reality is entirely different. And the bending and contorting we do often means that we find out too late that the game is rigged and our stories have been stolen.

I wrote about this in one of my rap songs:

Back in the days
I had a kingdom that was great.
Then you tried to come and take my moms on a date.
She didn't want to go so you dragged her down slow.
My pops would have bust you in the head but he didn't
    know.
Overwhelmed by the promise of the better life west.
Didn't know the promise excluded him and the rest.
He didn't smell the rat until it was too late,
the ones who refused hung in nooses
while the rest was chained.
But a chain is only as strong as its weakest link.
Stop the missing link is what you seek.
Don't blink.
Now you see.
Blink again and I'm gone like the wind.
Inshallah, I'll return four centuries from then.

This is my worry for Black youth today. Too many of us don't realize just how expendable we are. We're trapped in this cycle of wanting freedom but believing the lies told to us about who we inherently are. Some of us believe that jail is a rite of passage, and some simply see no other option. Too many young Black men, in essence, choose isolation and containment, a kind of death, rather than persisting in a world that denies them freedom anyway.

Maybe this is why so many in Black communities celebrate survival so much. Choosing to survive, to keep living, no matter what that looks like, makes the containment feel like an obstacle we've overcome. Many people come up to me and say they are so glad I survived. And I'm certainly grateful. There's something to be said about having survived these systems with my mental faculties still intact. But the truth is, not everyone shares my survival story, and so I ask: Where is their victory?

I've talked to many exonerees, and their emotional and mental struggles continue even after being freed. In that way, the Exonerated Five are fortunate. We get to tell our story. For those of us who choose to, we get to tell our story over and over and over again, and the power in giving our stories air means we get to heal over and over and over again. But many who were formerly incarcerated or recently exonerated—dare I say most—do not have that opportunity. Working with the Innocence Project has shown me this. Too many men and women who live with the grief from this particular experience don't have the opportunity to heal in the ways that I have been afforded. Most of the people who are home and free through the Innocence Project were found innocent because of the organization's relentless work. We were unable to benefit from that kind of advocacy. We came home through parole. We came home to the negativity that comes with being labeled as the scum of the earth. We came home wanting to hide. We made do with scrounging for any crumbs we could get, not making any noise. But when it came time for us to fight, we came together like a Voltron of brotherhood. We leaned on each other, and with the exoneration an astronomical change happened. We were now celebrated.

There's a photo of my mother with a sign that says "Yusef is innocent." She has the biggest, brightest, and most beautiful smile. My sister and a few friends are standing next to her. But my mother had always been and continued to be very skeptical when there was talk of our exoneration. She understood that the system was not going to give us our roses.

By 1999, I'd moved to Georgia. In my mind, New York represented evil. The city had caused me, my family, and our community so much pain. But meetings were happening. My mom held gatherings in the community center in her building to discuss the possibilities of our exoneration. Probably even more so than my mother, *I* was skeptical of the chance to be exonerated when Reyes was brought forth as the suspect. The system had already mishandled this case in such a bad way that, in my mind, I thought they were just going to cover themselves by saying he was the sixth man. I just knew we were going to have to live our lives with this indelible scar.

The media devoured us in 1989; more than four hundred articles had been written, ripping our lives apart. We were in the eye of the storm of public opinion and speculation, a storm that we weren't supposed to survive. In 1997 I came home to a world that still saw us as beasts that should be lynched. But in 2002, when we were finally exonerated, the general response was the equivalent of "My bad." My mother said it best. "It was such a whisper, I wonder if the rats in New York City even heard it." They screamed about our guilt and whispered about our innocence.

I was so angry about this. And even more than angry, I felt let down. I wanted *all* of my life back. I wanted people on the street to not say, "That's the guy from the Central Park Five," but "That's the guy who was wrongly accused." The response that we now receive today is what I wanted and needed back then.

Things shifted with the Ken Burns documentary. Ken, according to his words, actually believed that we had committed the crime. "We all believed it," he said. It wasn't until his daughter, Sarah, who was graduating from college, wrote a thesis paper on criminal justice and bumped into Raymond Santana that his opinion began to change. She began to write the story that became the book *The Central Park Five: A Chronicle of a City Wilding* and ultimately the Central Park Five documentary she made with her father.

One night in Connecticut, at the end of a screening for Ken Burns's documentary, we'd just finished the Q&A, and I prepared to move on to the next part of the evening. Then I saw a silver-haired, elderly man making his way down the aisle. He was coming directly toward me.

My first instinct was to be wary. Many people have long-held beliefs about us; many felt challenged by our truth. It was hard to tell who was who. When the man got to me, he extended his hand to shake mine. He was gentle, even comforting, but there was also an urgency to his grasp. It was one of those moments when the handshake went on for a touch too long. Just as I thought I should pull away, he spoke:

"You don't understand. I came here because I was trying to understand why my good friend Ken Burns was making a film about rapists."

I was stunned. My breath caught in my chest. But then I could see the remorse in his eyes and he went on.

"I didn't know. I'm so sorry. I just didn't know." His grip and handshake made sense now.

I thanked him.

I thanked him for his words because there were too many people who would not have apologized. They would not have had the courage to come up to me, shake my hand, and reveal what they had believed. I appreciated him for sharing not only this fact but, more important, his ownership of this realization that his previously held beliefs were wrong and harmful. It was such a heartening and powerful way to end an already wonderful night.

At the screening in Connecticut where the silver-haired man came up to me.

(Courtesy of Mark F. Conrad)

I innately understand why people who have been found innocent through organizations like the Innocence Project, and are happy to be home, are still devastated in some ways. They haven't been fully restored back into society. These accusations and convictions upend whole families, and it ripples down to devour entire communities. Pulling at the fibers that are Black and Brown families is bound to leave gaping holes in the fabric of the communities where they live.

And I can imagine that those who have been freed might

have felt like, "This has been happening all around. These men are five of hundreds of thousands. Where is our spotlight? What about us?" And they are right. Our story isn't new. It's the story of Alfred Chestnut, Ransom Watkins, and Andrew Stewart, wrongly convicted in 1983 in the Georgetown Starter jacket murder and exonerated thirty-six years later. It's the story of Ronnie Long, wrongly convicted in 1976 of robbing and raping a white woman in North Carolina by an all-white jury and exonerated forty-four years later, and too many others.

But to be clear, even with my privileges, the work is still hard and heavy. Financial compensation can never erase the emotional and physical scars that come with being run over by the system. The wounds, though healing, will, in certain ways, always feel fresh. When I see other people going through something similar, when the news breaks of another Black man being freed after serving thirty years for a crime he did not commit, something is shaken in me. It makes me want to fight for the truth. I raise my voice and ask, "How do we allow someone to have decades of their life stolen from them?" I want to scream for all who will hear that what we call the prison-industrial complex is simply a new and improved cotton field. And every generation that continues to buy into the lies and stereotypes of Black men and women as criminals will continue to provide bodies for those fields. As an educator and a mentor for a new generation, I am trying to fill the shoes of the mentors that I once had, imparting knowledge and raising the youth to consciousness, just as they did for me.

⚬⚬

There were so many people along the way who supplemented what my family and prison taught me with valuable knowledge that serves me to this day. There were numerous others who stood up for us despite the lies that were being told in the media. Bill Perkins, who later went on to be a New York City councilman and a state senator, was very vocal on our behalf.

You know these folks, you know us. You know my sons.

This is not them, this is not their character. Can you stand up for them?

His stance was always, "I'll help you and do everything I can." And behind the scenes, he did exactly that. After we came home and were revealed as innocent, especially after the Ken Burns *Central Park Five* documentary, he was still there standing with us. That was also when we got our first proclamation from the City of New York. Council members, including Charles Barron, signed the document that essentially said, "We are recognizing that these men are innocent. They should have never gone to prison. Regardless of what New York City is saying, we are going to recognize the truth." They took it upon themselves to revise the story that the city and media had been telling, and that was key in shifting the overall narrative.

Another significant person in my life at the time was my tutor during the trial, Helena Nomsa Brath, the wife of Elombe

I was always so grateful for the people who came to visit me. Left to right: The great Pan-African activist Elombe Brath, Shareef, my mom, and Mieasia.

Brath, the beloved Pan-African activist and founder of the Patrice Lumumba Coalition. Nomsa was a master teacher who was part of my community, my village. She said, "Okay. You can't be in school? We got you." My mother met Nomsa because they lived in our building prior to moving up to Adam Clayton Powell Jr. Boulevard. It was Nomsa who kept me reading and writing, in the same ways my mother did, with a focus on my African heritage. We explored texts like Ivan Van Sertima's *They Came Before Columbus* and others that focused on the role of the African Diaspora in civilization. More than anything else, learning with Nomsa provided a stabilizing presence for me when the rest of my life felt like it was exploding. I couldn't go to school, but going to her house kept my mind busy and focused.

I met Asia, my first girlfriend, while being tutored at the Braths'. The day that she walked into their home, I felt like my breath was stolen from my body. I was a typical teenage boy, so it was a physical attraction. But there was also something different about her, majestic. I've always been drawn to women who comport themselves in regal ways. It would also be Asia who would provide the link to another important teacher in my life.

We continued to date even after the trial and sentencing for about two years. While her support meant everything to me, I struggled with it. I learned pretty quickly that the longer I held on to love, the dream of it, the more difficult it would be for me to do my time. That tension was always present and very painful. She'd come to visit me while I was in the youth facility when she was home from college, and we'd write letters to each other. We'd talk about our love and desire in all the sappy ways teenagers and young adults do. She'd share with me everything that was going on in her world. But eventually, our relationship ended. It felt unfair to keep it going if, as I thought then, I would never get out of jail. I always try to maintain a positive outlook, but when the days begin to stretch longer in front of you and the years start to go by, it can become harder to see the end. I didn't like that helpless feeling of loving someone I couldn't hold. I was not going to be able to do my time well if I continued to try. I wrote to her and said, "Look, you know this ain't going to work. You should just move on without me."

I think she was confused by my reaction. Her response was essentially, "What do you mean?"

Asia McDonald

Soon after I came home from prison, I ran into Asia and asked, "How did life turn out?"

She replied, "I couldn't believe that you were telling me to leave. I was there. I was going to stay but you pushed me away."

Wow. A part of me was surprised to hear her say that. I had really just wanted to do the right thing by her and myself. What I couldn't explain at the time was that prison was teaching me some necessary lessons for survival. Remember "Do the time; don't let the time do you"? That was one of the most important assignments of my life. But it also meant that the love I had for Asia, any anticipation of what might lie ahead, had to be put aside; any wanting would have to be cut off. In that space, even the smallest of desires could send you spiraling emotionally.

Nevertheless, Asia and I remained friends, and I credit her with pointing me in the direction of one of my greatest teachers. Asia ended up going to Clark Atlanta University, a Historically Black College in Georgia, and eventually became a doctor with her own successful practice. About two years after I'd been back, she asked me one day, "Hey, listen, you want to go to college?"

I did. I'd been wanting to finish my bachelor's degree since before I was released. Her words were just the push I needed to go ahead and register at Hunter College.

Asia later said, "Look, there's a professor you need to meet at Hunter. Her name is Dona Richards."

The next time I was on campus, I went looking for the professor and I couldn't find her. This really bothered me. One of the biggest challenges I'd had after having seven years of my formative late teens and early adulthood stolen from me was the embarrassment of being an adult but having to ask for help with the simplest things. I was a grown man with a sixteen-year-old's mind-set, so some of the things that many people my age found easy I found to be complicated. The changes in the world from 1990 to 1997 felt overwhelming. It wasn't just that I saw new buildings and people walking with (by today's standard) huge mobile phones. My family and friends made sure to keep me up-to-date on those kinds of things. It was about having to navigate all that newness. It's one thing to hear about change or see photos of progress, but it's another to actually have to figure out how to move around among it all. The act of asking for a directory or stopping in an office to ask for assistance was so incredibly frustrating. Each day, after searching for Professor Richards, I'd resign myself and say, "Oh well. I'll look again tomorrow." Finally, after learning from Asia that she was in the Black and Puerto Rican Studies department, I got up the nerve to search the signage and office doors for her name.

I didn't see her name on any of them, either.

I thought I was losing it. *Why can't I find this person? What am I missing here?*

The next time I spoke to Asia, I told her about my search for Professor Dona Richards coming up empty. She said, "Oh, I think she changed her name. Her name is Marimba Ani."

Wait, what? I thought.

Dr. Marimba Ani was an anthropologist and African Studies scholar who coined the term *Maafa* to name the African holocaust / transatlantic slave trade. She was the protégée of the great thinker and scholar Dr. John Henrik Clarke.

When I returned to campus, I found Dr. Ani immediately, and it turned into one of the most profound experiences of my life. I didn't have any real intention when I crept into her class that day. I showed up because I was told that she was someone I should talk to, and I'm not sure I even realized that she'd be teaching at that moment. I didn't get a chance to take a seat when Dr. Ani, in the middle of teaching her class, looked at me as I was trying to silently enter the room. She moved closer to me, holding my gaze, and then gently placed both of her hands on my face.

"I knew you didn't do it."

My heart somersaulted. My body was filled with the warmth of her recognition.

Oh my goodness. Somebody knows.

Her touch was sincere and motherly. It felt like an invitation to life. How incredibly life-giving to be in a space where someone knew my journey, understood what was at stake, and publicly declared me innocent. It was a complete affirmation. Dr. Ani's compassion was a blessing. Her embrace anointed me for everything I'd do going forward. Those six words filled me with a sense of relief that I had not experienced before then. Those six words were a form of healing. Throughout this interaction, all of the students, peers, were watching and taking it all in. It never occurred to me to be embarrassed. The moment was too powerful for that. I suspect it was a powerful moment for them as well. One of those students was Ibi Zoboi, who went on to be an award-winning writer, and whom I'd ultimately partner with to write our young adult novel, *Punching the Air*.

I ended up auditing Dr. Ani's class, which wasn't something that happened often. Her classes always filled up quickly and had a long waiting list. Auditing was generally not an option, but she made an exception for me. She was also very selective about the students who did end up on her roster. On day one of class, Dr. Ani would say, "Look around. Half of you are not going to be here come next week." This wasn't because she was dropping students. They would drop out either when they saw the amount of work required or, to be frank, the type of information she shared would shake up everything a person had ever been taught about the power and legacy of people from the African Diaspora. Even though they all—white students, Black students—wanted this information, her position was: Not everybody gets it.

What I learned from Dr. Ani was monumental in shaping my understanding of who I am, who Black people are, and why Eurocentric systems and ways of living are problematic, at best. It also challenged me to be better at articulating what I was learning. It wasn't enough to just have these epiphanies while reading a book or having a discussion. She encouraged us to expound on these revelations. To be able to write about it. She knew whether you were getting what she was teaching by the way you expressed what you understood about it. Her textbooks weren't the classic books found in any bookstore. She'd bring Black booksellers into the classroom because the texts she wanted us to read were gems like *Facing Mount Kenya*, *The Isis Papers*, and *The Iceman Inheritance*. Her own book, *Yurugu*, deconstructed white supremacy and white male dominance in a way that was both challenging and beautiful. She defined white supremacy for us, even if we didn't call it by that name back then. She gave us the tools to really describe this oppression we were experiencing, that Black people had always experienced since the beginning.

Even my own faith tradition was challenged in her class. Students would say, "Oh, you know, Yusef. Islam is not an African way of life. It's Arabic." But in this environment, I was being taught to think critically. I learned to never take these challenges personally. What I know and believe about Islam does not have to align with what others believe. I believe Islam is the oldest faith. The prophets of the Jewish religion, like Abraham; and of Christianity, like John the Baptist, can be found in our texts. To others that belief may not resonate; it may not be accurate. That's perfectly fine. Because when I think about Islam, I think about the ways in which it saved me. The way the grace of Allah sheltered me when things could have gotten worse for me in prison.

That's not to say I didn't experience real danger. One time I awoke in the middle of the night to the whispering of officers' voices outside of my cell. "Oh, he's over there. Right there, on the top bunk." I moved a little, maybe even coughed, just so they'd know I was awake and would think twice about trying to do something to me.

There were other times when I would wake up around midnight and my cell would be open, just a little bit. It was dark and everyone was sleeping, so why exactly was the cell door open? On those nights, I'd get up, look out for a second, and close it. It made me feel like someone was trying to set me up. They were leaving the door open so someone could come and harm me and it would look like nobody knew what happened. Ultimately, nothing ever came of these events, and it felt like I was protected in ways beyond what I could see with my eyes.

My experience of grace reminds me of that story of Abraham (ع) the prophet found in both the Qur'an and the Bible.

Abraham (ع) was thrown into a fire by his enemies, but it was his enemies who got the shock of their lives.

> They said, "Who has done this to our gods? Indeed, he is of the wrongdoers."
>
> They said, "We heard a young man mention them who is called Abraham."
>
> They said, "Then bring him before the eyes of the people that they may testify."
>
> They said, "Have you done this to our gods, O Abraham?"
>
> He said, "Rather, this—the largest of them—did it, so ask them, if they should [be able to] speak."
>
> So they returned to [blaming] themselves and said [to each other], "Indeed, you are the wrongdoers."
>
> Then they reversed themselves, [saying], "You have already known that these do not speak!"
>
> He said, "Then do you worship instead of Allah that which does not benefit you at all or harm you?
>
> "Uff [Woe] to you and to what you worship instead of Allah. Then will you not use reason?"
>
> They said, "Burn him and support your gods—if you are to act."
>
> Allah said, "O fire, be coolness and safety upon Abraham."
>
> And they intended for him harm, but We made them the greatest losers.

And We delivered him and Lot to the land which We had blessed for the worlds.

And We gave him Isaac and Jacob in addition, and all [of them] We made righteous.

Qur'an 21:59–72

God said to the fire, "Be cool and safe."

That resonated so much with me. This idea that I could be in the fire, that the system and those who carry out the system's edicts could try every way possible to take me out, and in the midst of the fire, God called me to be cool and safe. Through Islam, I learned that in this life there are always spiritual things at work. And spiritual activity can be enacted by our very words. I learned that I could say things that could bring me into safety, in the same way I could say things that could bring harm upon me. That's part of the spiritual truth I believe in. It's not that you're just putting these words out there in the atmosphere, but you know that these words have weight. These words have value. These words have the ability to bring protection around you. There is power in our words.

In the youth facility, I was an Imam, the leader, the one to whom everyone said, "We receive our spiritual guidance from you." From that experience, I learned what it meant to advise and guide people. I learned how to research and study—teachings that are incredibly useful to me even to this day. Just like every other African American, I've been able to synthesize the knowledge of who I am as an African with my reality and experience as an American. I have needed to be able to do that in order to live.

So no matter how many times I was confronted with what people believed Islam was *not*, when folks challenged me to consider the glorious traditional African religions we were studying, I recognized that I'd been synthesizing. Making sense of what I was learning in concert with my current context and beliefs. I maintained my peace because I recognized that there were no purity tests in any faith tradition, only truth. From a spiritual perspective, anything dealing with true spirituality is Islam. Not the religion. For *Islam* simply means submitting yourself to God. I don't get to tell people which form or practice their submission should take. Moses (ع) submitted his will to God but didn't call the acts and tenets he employed Judaism. That came much later. Jesus (ع) submitted His will to God but didn't name His ministry Christianity. That came much later. But if we look at the essence of what spoke to these prophets and divine leaders, then you'll realize that at the core of it all, there is no difference. There is a Creator. And once you plug into that creative force and say, "Not my will, but Your will," that's when things take off. Whatever you might ultimately name it.

TEN

A Mother's Love

We delight in the beauty of the butterfly, but rarely admit the changes it has gone through to achieve that beauty.

MAYA ANGELOU

MY MOTHER RECEIVED SO MUCH hate mail during the trial, and for a long time afterward. Mail I never knew about until much later. She showed up for every court date and, later, every visit, always with a smile on her face—all the way up until the day I was released. In a way, we did time together. She, my brother and sister, and the rest of my family became the other prisoners in my story. Dealing with the media spectacle, holding me up, all while managing to have their own lives, was a challenge, and yet they continued to move forward. I had a strong village before prison—they were those powerful role models who loved me—and I had an even stronger, though deeply changed, village afterward.

I don't identify with language like "single-parent households," especially when I had such powerful guides like my uncle Frank, who was always right there beside me, loving me as I am. Or my aunt Denise, who was fly and smart and rarely said no to me. I had Frosted Flakes (with extra helpings of sugar) and no bedtime at her house. She was my mother's younger sister, and she encouraged my mother to stop calling me by her favorite love handle for me. "You got to stop calling that boy Baby."

I was loved well.

Kevin's sister, my mom, Kevin's mom, our friend and fellow inmate John Ball's mom, and John's sister Teresa, bringing food on a visit to Harlem Valley, through Mother Love.

Mom even found a way to come and cook for the prison. She created an organization called Mother Love and used it as an entry into the facility to cook for the inmates. I'm not sure how she made it happen. I know she'd built a connection with Dr. Leonard G. Dunston, who was running the Division of Youth at that time, and he was part of the same network as Elombe Brath. However she did it, everyone looked forward to the one or two days a year when she and her crew would come in. On those days, gone were the gray soups and suspicious meats. Her feasts felt like a Thanksgiving meal on steroids. She'd serve collard greens, mac and cheese, fried chicken, baked turkey, and all kinds of other sides. Everyone felt special that day, but I especially benefited. I became the guy whose mom would bring the feast. It gave me a kind of cool and garnered me respect inside. In truth, I think my mom just wanted to keep an eye on me, and this was the best way to do it.

She was what some would call overprotective. She was determined to provide us a safe harbor, shelter. For a long while, we didn't know any other way. She kept us safe within our village. At least as safe as a young boy in New York City could be, I suppose. And it was a delicate balance, because she wasn't trying to prevent me from growing up. But no matter how old I get, I'll always be her baby. Though, to Aunt Denise's point, words matter. Especially how we use them. Having felt protected by my mother my entire childhood made the tragedy of going to prison much more painful. I suspect it felt the same for her. With the myriad of ways she kept me and my brother and sister out of harm's way, she taught us all the things we needed to know. But she couldn't ultimately protect me from being run over by injustice. I know that pierces her heart to this day.

Mom uses words to speak wisdom and truth. And she is also funny. Not like a comedian, but just as someone who can talk about life in a way that is articulate, highlighting its joys and absurdities, with a turn of phrase that makes her observations unintentionally hilarious. And she never curses. Coarse language was never used inside our home.

"Yo, your mother is hilarious," everyone would say. "You must get it from her."

I don't think either one of us thought we were funny. We were rarely trying to be. From my mother, I learned to say it like I saw it, to be real about everything. Her tone was always matter-of-fact, and I think I've taken on some of that. Her influence flows through me when I'm onstage and I'm telling my story.

When I was young and would be playing around with my friends, I'd slip and curse every now and again, but it was mostly me trying to act like the people I saw in the neighborhood or at school. In prison, however, I learned that cursing was a tactic that people used when they didn't know how to express themselves. It reinforced what my mother taught me. When I learned the power of the words we speak, I stopped cursing.

Up until I was around ten years old, Mom wore a full hijab when we went out. She didn't shield her face, but she honored the verse in the Qur'an that says, "O Prophet, tell your wives and your daughters and the women of the believers to bring down over themselves [part] of their outer garments" (33:59). In a strange way, when she was fully covered, I felt protected. I could hide behind her cloak, so to speak. She loves to tell stories about how we would go to the grocery store together. Usually other kids would eat a handful of grapes while their mother shopped. Not me. Mom says I ate half the bananas in the basket before we even got to the cashier line. Now mind you, these were the real, non-GMO bananas, the ones that still have the black seeds in them. When you walked by the produce stand, you could smell the fruit strong and inviting. Even though I ate them before we paid for them, she never was angry with me about it. She was my shield. If her baby was hungry, he ate.

Growing up uptown, it was common to hear folks shooting fireworks on the Fourth of July or on New Year's Eve. In the hood, these weren't "oh, look how beautiful" types of explosives. At least not in the eyes of a child. Around my way, people didn't always just shoot fireworks in the sky. They sometimes shot them at people. So the popping sounds and loud booms, to me

as a little kid, were terrifying. But my mom, as always, knew how to calm my spirit. She would find a way to shift my fear into wonderment. "Wow, look at that!" Even if it didn't always work and I was still scared, her words, her voice didn't allow my fear to expand into terror.

My mother raised us mostly vegan. We rarely ate meat. And we didn't find it uncomfortable because we didn't know anything different. When we drank milk, it was goat's milk. And, of course, almost everything we ate, Mom made. She fed us using the eating principles found in *Back to Eden*, a book that explores the use of herbs, healthy foods, and other holistic practices. In fact, our entire family eating plan was based on this book. When we ate bread, we ate bread my mother made. When we wanted cookies, we ate the cookies she baked. If we wanted yogurt, she churned the yogurt from scratch. To this day, before I eat anything, my first question is "What's in this?" She taught us the importance of putting healthy things in our bodies. Staying well for the fight.

This would also be useful later when she began to experience her own health challenges. When my mother developed Stage 4 cancer, her first step toward healing, after surgery, was returning to her *Back to Eden* diet. She's now a three-time cancer survivor.

Because Mom worked long hours at Parsons, we had to learn how to cook as young children. She taught us how to make rice and, when we weren't vegan, the occasional lamb chops. Despite our mostly plant-based diet, I even learned how to season and cook chicken. We didn't often eat together—three teens in the house with a working mother meant a busy schedule. On the day I got locked up, I had those lamb chops baking in the oven. I remember my sister being so angry because she knew I hadn't eaten anything. I was a growing boy with a healthy appetite. It was nothing for me to put away a whole plate of vegetables and then chase it with a whole plate of spaghetti. That was how I ate. On the day I was arrested, it didn't occur to me that I had eaten my last meal the night before.

Family is important. Love is critical. Those were the principles we lived by. We were taught to not concern ourselves as

Holidays at home.

much with what people called us. My mother wasn't a single mother. She was a mom who worked. We weren't kids without a dad. We were kids who had a whole village of dads. My uncle was my father figure. Whenever he did things with Frank, his son and my cousin, I was always right there with them. I was thankful to have my uncle in my life, because he was truly like a parent to me. And because me and my cousin are so close and so connected, I'd always hang out with them.

But this didn't stop me from thinking about my own father. Wondering why he left. Dreaming that he'd come visit us or maybe even come back for good. But I chose to focus on what was in front of me. I had a fatherly presence there, just not in my household. When I'd hang out with my uncle, there were times I felt envious, despite being so loved on by him and his family. Maybe it was jealousy. Maybe it was just awe at their relationship. Perhaps it was both. But there were moments when the wanting in my heart, that gulf, was widened from watching their interactions.

Wow, Frank has his dad. He can go home to his dad. I don't. I can't.

I never saw my mother with a man. She had male friends, but I never suspected, never said, "Oh, that's Ma's boo." We were never introduced to anyone with "Oh, this is your uncle." You know how everybody has those new "uncles," right? I suppose this was another of the many ways my mother protected us. I don't know for sure if she had any romantic relationships, but I know we didn't see them. No one was going to intrude on our family dynamic. She believed in stability; that was what she was determined to give us, and she did.

What I love most about my mother is she's a no-nonsense kind of person. As I watched Aunjanue Ellis's portrayal of her in *When They See Us*, I said to myself, *Oh shucks, that's my mom!* Aunjanue nailed it. She was beyond excellent. My mother is fierce and fearless in the face of injustice. In fact, my mom got arrested one time when I was a little boy. It was the most noble, honorable arrest, in my eyes.

Back in the '80s, there were so many fires in the Schomburg Plaza buildings where we lived. It didn't seem like anyone cared about our safety. In March 1987, there was an incredibly tragic fire in which seven people died, including three young people who jumped to their deaths in a vain attempt to escape. I knew them. In an incredible twist, fire dispatchers had assured those calling as the fire and smoke took hold that it was under control.

When the next bad fire rolled around, a man named Daoude Woods took action. Daoude was well over six feet tall, his eyes dark with determination. He just exuded strength. To look at him was to see raw power. During this particular fire, Daoude was racing in and out of the buildings, helping to get people out. When the fire department came, they tried to stop him, even though he told them there was an old man trapped on one of the higher floors. "I need to get him. I know he's there. I got to go get him."

The firefighter responded, "You cannot go in the building."

Daoude shrugged. "Y'all going to have to do what y'all got to do."

When they tried to block him, he knocked one of the firemen down and ran into the building. Many excruciating minutes later, he came running back out, carrying that older gentleman on his shoulders. The courtyard erupted in cheers, full of admiration for Daoude and the selfless act we'd just witnessed.

The police arrived and were not as impressed. When they arrested Daoude, he didn't fight it. It was clear that he was just grateful to be able to save the people he did. He was like, "Okay, cool, no problem. Arrest me. I had to save that man and I'll go back and save more if you let me." They put him in the back of the squad car parked in the circular driveway. Then the cops climbed into the backseat and repeatedly punched our hand-cuffed hero. With everyone watching.

Then my mother jumped into the fray.

"Let him go, let him go!" she led us in a chant.

From there it turned into total mayhem, with the police snatching all kinds of folks.

"Let him go, let him go!"

Practically every Plaza tenant joined in, with everyone, including my mother, shaking the cop car. That was when she was arrested.

They took her to the jail on 103rd Street between Third and Lexington. When we arrived, we found her handcuffed to the wall.

I never told my mother about lying on my coat that first night at the precinct after they took us all in, but I suspect if I had, she would have known what I was feeling. The idea of being righteous and standing for your truth while paying the price for it was likely familiar to her. All she ever tried to do was protect her family and her community.

There were many heroes like Daoude and my mother in my neighborhood. Korey Wise saved a man's life once. When one of our neighbors was going to jump off his balcony in a suicide attempt, Korey showed up to the man's unit, gently talked him down off the ledge, and convinced him to come back inside his house. That incident was high-profile and dramatic, and I'm sure it was covered by the newspapers. People like Daoude and Korey were *our* heroes.

With my grandmother at graduation.

During the thick of the fighting for justice for me, Mom was naturally stressed and stretched thin. Most people would have reached for a drink or ten to take the edge off, but that wasn't my mother's way. She'd tasted alcohol only one time in her life, when she was young. She told her mom, who would occasionally have a drink, "I want to taste that." So my grandmother made an especially disgusting version of a cocktail and passed it to her daughter.

My mom took one sip. "Ugh! This is nasty. I'm never drinking that mess again." And she didn't.

When things were at their craziest, and Mom was trying to hold it together, one of my relatives said they wished my grandmother had given her a sweeter drink way back then. Maybe she'd have an easier time coping. My mother was certainly the glue that kept my hopes alive while we were at trial. But I often wondered what she did for herself. When did she lay her cape down, if ever?

I struggle with calling my mother a superhero, not because she isn't one, but after all that she's lived through, she deserves to be able to rest. Black women are often saddled with the "strong Black woman" trope, and it can undermine their humanity. We have tasked Black women with the pressure to play this part of the superwoman, a protective measure in order to cope with the constant stressors of racial discrimination. Yes, they are resilient. Yes, they seem to come to the aid of the whole world. But Black women cry. They feel. They grieve. They hurt. They deserve their own healing. My mother deserves her healing.

Even when things were out of her control, when the system literally stole me right out from under her, I knew that my mother would always be there fighting for me. Everything about her always made me feel safe. I just want her to feel the same. Patrisse Khan-Cullors, cofounder of the Black Lives Matter movement and author of the memoir *When They Call You a Terrorist*, captures the feelings that I know still explode my mother's heart to this day:

Is this what it is to be a mother who has to carry the weight of having to protect her children in a world that is conspiring to kill them? Are you forced to exist within a terrible trinary of emotion: rage, grief or guilt? What of the joy and the peace that loving a child brings? What of pride and of hope? Could it really be true that my mother has been given no door number four or five or six or even seven to walk through in order to know the wholeness of motherhood? Is she one in a long line of Black mothers limited to survival mode or grief?

Mama is my Harriet Tubman, yes, but she is also Joanne Chesimard. She is also Angela Davis. All of these women, these sheroes, are examples for her of how not to go down without a fight. But now, I want her to rest.

○∼

Our family was known to be close-knit. While we were involved in acts of "good trouble," as the late congressman John Lewis called it, for the most part we lived quiet lives. Then suddenly we were placed in the middle of a major crime and media circus. While I was the one facing conviction, what was happening to me was happening to all of us. In light of the worst trouble ever, the only lawyer my mother found who was willing to take up our case was a divorce attorney.

Mom met Robert Burns through a family friend. I didn't

know the difference between a criminal defense attorney and a divorce attorney. In my mind, they all went to law school. They all sat for the bar exam. They all received licensing credentials from the state. To me and my family, that meant they were equally credible.

The court of public opinion disagreed. They viciously attacked Robert, claiming he wasn't worth his salt. We had no way to gauge a good attorney from a bad one. We also didn't have much money. Yet when Mom called on him to help, he answered. He was the only one who stood up to represent us before the judge.

She met with Robert at a bar. Desperate and exhausted, she recounted how she'd come home from work to find my sister, Aisha, frantic. "They took Yusef!" No one knew how to find me. The whole situation was so unreal that she actually thought my sister and I were playing a joke on her. She walked around the house, crawling on the floor, searching underneath the couch and then under the bed. She thought I was hiding.

The police did not come here and take my boy.

When she realized that it wasn't a joke but everything she had ever feared, she got herself to the precinct.

The hardship that my mother endured that night, beginning with the cruel treatment she experienced at the hands of the police officers, simply for trying to find out basic information about my whereabouts and charges, is the reason we believe she got cancer. I know what that sounds like. But as Bessel Van der Kolk describes in *The Body Keeps the Score*: "Long after a traumatic experience is over, it may be reactivated at the slightest hint of danger and mobilize disturbed brain circuits and secrete massive amounts of stress hormones." Stress hormones impact the body's ability to fight off a number of illnesses.

My mother encountered a sick justice system, and that sickness was contagious. How does a mother engage self-care under these terms? A massage at a fancy spa was not the answer. And because there weren't any easy answers, not to mention the Goliath we encountered in the justice system, we believe all that worry and anxiety likely metastasized into cancer. We would eventually slay that giant, but not before it did its best to slay us.

Very few things comforted Mom when I went to trial and was later sentenced. She grieved heavily for me. She feared for my safety. She worried that injustice would win. Instead of sitting idle on the sidelines, she founded her nonprofit Mother Love, now called People United for Children. But it wasn't just my mom and me going through the fire—it was our whole village. While one mother can do a little bit, a "people united for children" can wield incredible power. She began to research how the system worked, then began to teach others how to work the system. That was how she learned about opportunities for people to serve inmates and was able to work as a cook at the facility. Our bodies were imprisoned, but every year, thanks to my mom, we went *Back to Eden*. It was another moment of mental freedom driven by her love.

When people are trying to paint a picture of you, when they are trying to assess if you're worthy of justice, they poke around your influences, beginning in your early home life. Our home was orderly, and my mother was no-nonsense. We were typically good kids who did regular kids' stuff, usually nothing serious. But if we got into trouble that was bad enough to require a spanking, it was rough. First, we'd be told to take off our clothes, because my mom knew that we would try to outwit her by wearing multiple layers. Eventually we learned it was easier to obey.

I've never been able to get a clear read on the impact my incarceration had on my siblings. With Aisha, she was always so present. If you look at pictures from back then, you'll see my sister in all of those pictures. Honestly, we've never really talked about how my conviction has affected her in her adult life. But just like a lot of other sisters, like many Black women today, she was always out front and center making her voice heard about my innocence. She never shied away from a camera in shame or embarrassment. She was always there. My brother, less so. I think my mother was shielding Shareef a lot from what was happening. One of Shareef's best friends clued me in to how painful my being sent away must have been for him. One day during the trial when they were in class, the teacher brought in a newspaper. I was on the front cover. She pointed at Shareef and announced, "That's Yusef Salaam's brother."

"Man, your brother just put his head down, in shame, wanting to hide and all of that."

It never escaped me that we were all prisoners of this system. My brother had his way of dealing with it. My sister had hers. Neither discussed with me how they were faring. And my mother, who took the brunt of everything, had her own way. She carried it all. She was out there all the time with me in the world.

Mom's brilliance was only matched, in my mind, by her loving kindness and passion. While she never opened an official business, my mother used her expertise as a seamstress and fashion designer to serve our village and others in our community. She made clothes for various people on the side and even designed and constructed my sister's beautiful, intricate wedding dress. Many of the dresses she wore herself were created by her own hand. In addition to teaching fashion design at Parsons, she taught us her trade at home, and taught the community children. I learned how to design clothes from her, my first accomplishment being a dress trench coat I'd wear often.

After the trial, she couldn't work anymore because they fired her, and in fact, she never worked again. She was deeply embedded in the grassroots organizations she started, relying on them and Social Security. She had a real entrepreneurial streak, and she could have been or done anything she would have wanted, but things came in her path, and life went in a different direction.

In light of all of this, it still never occurred to me as I was going through my experience pre-exoneration that my life was really indicative of the duality that W. E. B. Du Bois talks about in *The Souls of Black Folk*: "One ever feels his twoness,—an American, a Negro; two souls, two thoughts, two unreconciled strivings; two warring ideals in one dark body, whose dogged strength alone keeps it from being torn asunder."

My life reflected two parallel experiences. One of me doing everything I could to be a good son. The other being a distorted image of myself that lived in white people's imaginations.

I grew up in New York and my mother grew up in Alabama. Yet there we were, experiencing a similar oppression: my Black body being loved dearly by my people and simultaneously reviled in light of white supremacy being the order of things. Dr. James Baldwin—though it's not his official title, I consider him a doctor because of all he did with his words to heal the psyches of Black people—said that to be Black and relatively conscious "is to be in a state of rage all the time." That's what I think lay beneath all of the work, all of the protecting, and yes, all of the love my mother poured out. A soft but steady rage at the way Black people have been treated in this country. That burning was and is her motivation. It is also mine.

The key to surviving the simmering rage, to not letting it implode your insides, is to find outlets of service and creativity. Both my mother and I learned how to control our mental and emotional capacities and faculties so that our bodies didn't go where our minds were trying to drive them.

Ultimately, I am in control of my life. The galvanizing love I've been able to experience, and learning *how* to navigate through the many injustices I've faced—including all the ways a white supremacist system tried to get me to surrender—has undergirded any social justice work I've done. I learned that if you don't identify your rage and wield it wisely, you'll feel lost at best. At worst, your joy will escape you. Peace will pass you by.

This is what I had to remember when I was told that I was going to be doing my time at Brookwood (a relative country club, compared to other facilities) but ended up at the worst maximum-security facility there was: Harlem Valley. It's what I had to remember when I was forced out of the car in chains from wrists to ankles. My arms were shackled to the leather belt around my waist, with a chain going down to my ankles that caused me to stumble as I walked. I looked up at the large concrete building of the facility in front of me, and the fear I felt knocked the breath right out of me. I thought the walls were moving, vibrating against a pitch-black sky. And they were, in a way. Because just like back in the Tombs, the inmates were literally shaking the bars and fences, yelling, "We're going to get you! We're going to get you when you get in here!"

A constant state of rage.

My mama wasn't there to protect me anymore. I had to accept that. There was no flowing cloak to hide behind. There were no bananas to savor. No clean language and lamb chops.

No naked spankings. No kind words to defuse the frightening sounds of fireworks. And yet she was still there. Her words of affirmation were embedded in my heart. The tenets of her faith flooded and fortified my spirit. Her resistance, her fight, was very much alive in me. I stepped into that building not knowing what awaited me but definitely knowing who and what I was bringing in.

ELEVEN

Ignorance as a Trillion-Dollar Industry

If I didn't define myself for myself, I would be
crunched into other people's fantasies for me
and eaten alive.

AUDRE LORDE

One of my first public speaking engagements was as a member of the
Campaign to End the Death Penalty at the National Black Theatre in New
York City.

SOMETIMES IT'S OUR PERCEPTION OF prison that gets in the way. We have limitless power in Black and Brown communities. To harvest it, however, we must refuse to participate in our own degradation. When we understand history, specifically the loophole in the Thirteenth Amendment, we'll smash the prison-industrial complex and construct in its place a system that lives into our highest ideals: freedom and justice for all.

I grew up around guys from the block who went to jail. We'd see them taken away for one reason or another. Then they'd arrive home, chests large but eyes blank. It felt like they were returning prisoners of war. Some people celebrated their release with parties and small gifts. But strangely, they never talked with any depth about their experiences. The moments they did share, unfortunately, perpetuated the idea that jail was cool. They bragged about "running" the jail. About surviving it. But no one ever mentioned the other side: the loss of their right to vote, the challenge in getting a job and building a career outside of the streets, the emotional trauma and PTSD-like episodes. They had muscles and hood notoriety, but not much else.

No one in my family or immediate circle had ever gone to

jail. It was always the guy I knew from the neighborhood. Men I'd see at a distance while walking with my mom or siblings to the masjid or the store. When I became the one to go to prison, I finally understood what I was seeing in them.

Harlem Valley, where I ended up after my brief time in Spofford, was a maximum-security facility for youth. The inmates there included killers, rapists, and those charged with other extremely violent crimes, all committed by boys under the age of twenty-one. Some of their crimes would have sent them to Rikers Island or Clinton, but because they were convicted when under the age of sixteen, they were sent to Harlem Valley. Though it housed young men who *had* committed vile acts—and many who hadn't—it was Harlem Valley itself, the dehumanization seen there, that was evil at its core. The space carried a spirit that was unaligned with promoting healing and restoring youth offenders. Fortunately, it no longer exists.

Visits felt like a lifeline. Luckily Harlem Valley was relatively close by, a two-hour drive. While I was at Harlem Valley, my mom would visit me as often as possible, sometimes even one to two times a week. If there was a visitors' day on both Saturday and Sunday, she would find a way to stay somewhere overnight, in a hotel, so that she could be there each day. Her visits to me were a part of her process of taking care of me and making sure I was okay, while also taking care of herself. This was her way of living her life and coping with the loss of her secondborn. Prison doesn't affect just the incarcerated but changes and shapes the lives of everyone around that person.

You could tell the men who didn't have visits—they carried themselves with a certain kind of pain and anger. Many people had only their mother come; not very often did you see a mother and father, and even more rare was a father visiting on his own. Kevin and I would have lots of visitors. I had my mother, my brother, my sister, my cousins. People from the community would come to see Kevin, and then stop by to visit with me as well. We always had our people around us.

There were less visits at Clinton, where visits were set on a biweekly schedule based on your last name. When I arrived, because of where my name fit on that schedule, I had to wait almost a month until I got my first visit. I was overwhelmed with how long I wasn't able to see my family; it felt like I was going through withdrawal.

People often refer to the prison-industrial complex as *the belly of the beast*. My experience with the American justice system was like the birthing process in reverse. Going from the nurturing space of my mother's womb—the safety she tried so desperately to give me—to another womb, the birthing place of America's evil. The impact of that journey on me physically, spiritually, and mentally was significant—an unnatural process designed to malign and deform.

If the justice system is meant to ensure that criminals pay for their crimes, the current setup penalizes defendants two, three, and four times—beyond what is humane. True reform gives them the opportunity to return to society. True reform includes opportunities for rehabilitation—the kind that includes addressing the psychological and emotional needs and challenges of brothers and sisters coming out of jail. True reform would mean they feel safe and secure to be vulnerable when they need to. They might have had trauma before jail, and then experienced it while imprisoned, but when they leave they are able to safely and healthily release the fruit of that trauma—whether that's anger, sorrow, or whatever—from their minds and bodies.

Rehabilitation looks at the crime by examining the circumstances around it from different perspectives. A deep dive into the catalyst for a person's actions—likely trauma—is what makes a productive return to society a possibility instead of a pipe dream. My fellow inmates at Harlem Valley entered prison as children. They exited as children in adult bodies. Real reform requires us to peel the layers and get to core issues. Self-love and self-determination are possible, but not if the only thing we've experienced is the consistent message that our lives are worthless, and we internalize that message.

Raymond said something in the *Central Park Five* documentary that I'll never forget. I'm not sure I ever understood this about myself until he articulated it.

"It's like you come back home with all of these things that you didn't go into prison with."

To Raymond's point, some folks came home physically bigger but mentally and emotionally smaller. I came home and realized that despite all the grace I'd experienced, I was still institutionalized. Negativity burgeoned around my edges. I responded to everything in my world with suspicion. I felt like a rocket trying to exit the earth's atmosphere. I was trying to fly but the gravitational force that is negativity kept pulling me down. Sure, once I got the lessons my life was teaching me, I could lean back on the throttle, but that was going to take some serious unpacking.

When I got home and I began to plow my way forward, trying to get back to myself, I realized that I had an aversion to time. Perhaps because I had *done* time. Inside, every minute of my day was scheduled and accounted for. I had to relearn and regain a healthy relationship to how I used the hours I had. Today that looks like forcing myself to think that I have no time in order to be on time. I often pad my alarm or ask for people to give me a start time an hour before they actually need me. There's a powerful statement in Islam that says, "Time is like a sword. If you don't learn how to cut it, it will cut you." That was a guiding principle for me for a long time.

It's interesting how different cultures see or value time. In the Black community, we have "CP time," or "colored people's time," which essentially means we're late according to current societal values. The European construct for time is weighted differently than in many non-Western cultures. For example, the New York subway has a schedule, and people set their arrival and departure times based on the countdown timer on the platform. It is expected to arrive on time. When it doesn't, people are frustrated. In contrast, if you go to Jamaica, for example, and ask, "What time is the bus coming?" the running joke is "It soon come." The bus finally arrives an hour later, and on the side of the bus is the sign "Soon Come Bus." There's nothing inherently wrong with the "soon come bus." Their life patterns are built more around enjoying the moment. They have a sense of presence that is lost in Western cultures. Time is a distraction. It all comes soon.

I served time. Now my whole relationship to time had to be redrawn. That was one of the first lessons I learned with Dr. Marimba Ani. She helped me to unpack the notion of time as a construct, and those ideas fed my soul. She was such a luminary figure—in my life and the world—and she helped me. In the movie *Sankofa*, the main character goes through the Sankofa experience, and a woman looks at her with piercing, glorious eyes and says, "Yes, now you understand." Dr. Ani's influence on me was similar.

So much of the work I had to do post-release to unravel myself from the institutionalization was about awakening into the truth and the reality of where I was, why I was, and what I was. Of course, my identity is not only that I'm a Black man. But by definition of being a Black man, I was born into the struggle of fighting on the right side. As Ibram X. Kendi wrote in his popular book *How to Be an Antiracist*, "We were unarmed, but we knew that Blackness armed us even though we had no guns."

At every turn, I chose to buck the system. I chose to "not participate," as my mother told me early on. I chose not to capitulate to a false statement of who I was. I did all this even though I couldn't explain why. Yes, there's value in learning how to operate within their systems, as learning how to navigate the murky waters of oppression is something that many must do to survive. But it is equally important to know the truth. We have to be able to hold both of these realities. This dichotomy of living in two separate worlds that are running parallel is real. There is my definitive, unquestionable truth, and there is theirs.

This perspective comes at a cost, though. Once you begin to espouse and exhibit excellence and brilliance, telling people to go free, you're a problem. You could be LeBron James, but as soon as you start telling people Black lives matter, you're told to shut up and dribble. Too many people seek the validation of white people as a collective. They seek validation outside of themselves. Dr. Ani taught me that I don't need to be validated by any of these white folks. I am great and I come from greatness. But when you don't know who you are, you'll find yourself conforming to the image of yourself that best suits them. Our ignorance is a trillion-dollar business to them. Dr. Ani once said, "If you decided tomorrow that their system should cease to exist, tomorrow their system will cease to exist." Then she said, "Do you know what that's called? It's called power."

When you think about the worst atrocities that happened in human history, but most definitely what happened in the transatlantic slave trade, many people think about the resilience of our people. The ways in which they were able to endure and survive that many-generations-long bondage. The truth is: They were stronger than we could ever imagine. It was not about weakness. It was about survival. And it was about retaining a level of humanity within themselves, a part of themselves that always believed that better was coming. We have access to all of that. It's in our DNA.

Part of the concept of *all power to the people* introduced by many of the liberation movements of old is the understanding that we really, truly *do* have the power. We really do have a kind of sovereignty. There is de facto sovereignty and de jure sovereignty. The former suggests something is true even if it's not acknowledged or sanctioned, and the latter is something—a state of affairs—that aligns with the law. And yes, these terms are generally used politically in reference to the independence of nations, but in many ways they are very applicable to our own independence as Black people. There is a power that we have, which isn't sanctioned by these systems, and that's the power we need to wield in order to effect change.

It isn't easy to break out of the gravitational pull designed to keep us constrained. But we must find our way out, some way, somehow.

I recall the introduction of an old book I have saying that "Islam stands for change." I love that phrasing but want to switch it up a bit. Let's say that freedom stands for change also. True freedom, true liberation, means not just change for the oppressor, which is mandatory, but also change for the oppressed. Freedom seeks to change the individual, the society, and everything around us. And that's why there's so much opposition to our freedom from the outside and within. The kinds of psychological and spiritual shifts required by our liberation create enormous discomfort, and that resistance to discomfort drives the status quo. John Henrik Clarke said, "Every single thing that touches your life, religious, socially and politically, must be an instrument of your liberation or you must throw it into the ashcan of history." Those words reverberate in my soul. I've had to use everything in my life, the good, bad, and ugly, for the service of my freedom.

The hard reality is that in the process of trying to liberate ourselves, some of us will lose our lives. The same as those who died on the Middle Passage during uprisings or on plantations during rebellions or behind the billy club of a policeman during marches. But if we truly believe in justice and equality, what other choice is there?

I have power. We have power. But that power works better as a collective. It works best in unity.

Justice isn't hard to fathom, but for some, it feels like a pipe dream. We read in our history books about the founding fathers and their great dream for democracy. But we also know deep down that our oppressors across generations were saying, "Man, I got away with it all. I lived the good life on the backs on these people. I stole their land and money. I chopped up babies and fed them to alligators." We are disgusted and justice feels like a fruitless endeavor. But we forget that none of it is about truth and righteous living. It's only about telling the best story.

It's a spiritual wickedness in high and low places, as the elders say. Justice calls out to us to imagine an unseen reality. Yes, it's hard to fight air when the only evidence you have of its existence is the movement of the trees. It's hard to fight injustice when all we can see is the awful manifestations of it. But we must.

Together.

We've seen the destruction created by division. The Willie Lynch letter, a document believed to be a hoax that outlined the way slave masters would divide the enslaved by color in order to quell rebellion, still rings true based on what we see happening in our communities. The "divide and conquer" methodology, as old as time, is effective but not definitive. It's time to harness our power.

We know the destruction of oppression but have not yet been able to move out of its grasp. Our oppressors have mastered planning. Their moves have benefited multiple generations, which is why mass incarceration—slavery by another name—continues to exist. In order to defeat these generations-long plans of white supremacy, we must plan far ahead. The system depends on limited thinking from us, because they embedded it as a way of life. There was a time when we couldn't plan past the next day. To plan for a future when our children could be taken away from us next week, or when our significant others could be snatched away and sent down the Natchez River to Mississippi or into Alabama, felt senseless. The idea of building generational wealth feels unattainable when it's difficult to earn enough to serve your basic needs. So, yes, some of us will treat ourselves with Jordans or immerse ourselves in seemingly trivial things like the latest release by our favorite singer or rapper. Because we are human and not afforded much pleasure. And rightfully, that pleasure feels good to us in the midst of darkness. Thinking further out when everything around you says you might not live to see the fruits of your labor is the challenge. In Islam, we believe in justice. Not the kind of justice reflected in this country's systems. We believe in true justice wielded by God to heal us all. Maybe you call it "karma" or "reaping what you sow." No matter what, it's the concept we must embrace for our liberation. It's the African ethos of understanding that our ancestors have prepared a space for us in this world and the next. Our ability to unite and reframe the narrative can be the force that drives away the fear many of us hold, fear of the impossible.

Fear is dispelled when you realize that everyone is finite. Everyone wants to live a million years, but we know we cannot. So, part of the collective lack of intergenerational planning is rooted in this myth that "if I do that, they will kill me." And given history, on the one hand, it's a reasonable perspective. We know what happened to the Black people living on Black Wall Street in the Greenwood district of Tulsa, Oklahoma, one of the wealthiest Black neighborhoods in America. In 1921, those homes and businesses were burned to the ground by white people who couldn't stand that these formerly enslaved men and women were now thriving in a town of their own creation, with businesses, schools, and hospitals all run by Black people. Their success was an affront to that town's notions of supremacy. They killed those people as a way of blocking any attempt at "planning ahead."

I wrote in a poem once, "Everybody dies, but not everybody

lives. My God, I had my soul to give." There will, without a doubt, be a sacrifice. But we must play the long game. While I sat in my jail cell, I had to focus on the minute, the hour, and the day in order to survive. But after I was released, I had to slowly unravel from that framework. I had to think beyond that, to think about my family, the one I had, and the one I would have eventually. The journey of freedom for Black people is clearly a marathon, but it is also a relay. In our deaths, we pass the baton. Packaged in that DNA baton is the love, joy, pain, and trauma we pass on to the next generation, and the nourishment our children need is already planted inside them.

I know that many of us are just waiting for heaven. We are waiting for another plane of existence where oppression doesn't exist. We've been told that heaven is out there, above the sky Islamically; there's a belief in that. In one form or another, most belief systems ascribe to this. But it's hard to hold that fully when we look around us and see others seemingly enjoying their heaven here on earth. When I'd walk around Harlem and see the changes wrought by gentrification, it was hard to not wonder why the cleaner streets and renovated buildings couldn't have come earlier. But even as we fight to right the wrongs done to us, we must also release ourselves from what we've been taught has value. We must release the definitions given to us and stand firmly in who we know ourselves to truly be. That's where our "heaven on earth" lies. We can have the fly homes and cars. We can build up our neighborhoods and watch over our children. We can also be healthy, healed, and whole, despite the journey it takes to get there.

I recently saw an interview with a man from Bosnia. His children were translating for him. He knew the language that they were speaking—I believe it was German—but he essentially said he refused to speak the language of the colonizer. *He* was going to speak only in the language of his identity, Arabic. The tongue that would best express what he knew about himself and his experience. And this extends beyond linguistics. To his point, when we speak the cultural language of our oppressors, we will find ourselves thinking in the cultural language of our oppressors. When we can speak freely in our own tongue, we can think freely. While there's something to be said about leaving your words up to someone else's translation, what was also powerful to me was that this man didn't care.

I imagine that's what it looks like to retain ownership of self. To be exactly who you are, and let other people expend the labor to translate. Black people defining themselves for themselves and letting white people catch up is absolutely a power move. We are putting the onus back where it belongs. You do the labor, justice system, of undoing the horrors you've enacted. You do the work of dismantling this thing you've created, and I will reclaim and retain myself.

∽

There is a huge deficit in our Black and Brown communities that has been intentionally exploited by a culture and its systems determined to deny our humanity. As a result, some of us deal with a plague on our psyches. When who *we* are is too indelibly linked to how *they* see us, we are in trouble. I'd submit that we can trace all of it to a kind of love famine. We don't know how to love each other because we don't know how to love ourselves. We've lived so long in a place of survival that the idea of thriving in love and joy feels unattainable at best. Seeds of self-hate sowed by a country bent on denying you basic human rights can create a hate harvest that is sadly plentiful in Black and Brown communities. It's not about crime. People aren't robbing and shooting and dealing drugs because it's fun. Not even because it's cool. It's because their options are limited and their vision of themselves as whole and healed—as self-actualized—is cloudy. It's about a lack of self-love and identity.

To echo Malcolm X, the white man is the greatest criminal in the world, the greatest thief. The privileged have looted both natural and human resources globally. Even though Black people are resilient, though we are people equipped to survive, loving and being loved well is a stolen treasure. Too many of us can be prisoners of limited thinking, faithful students of our captors, who teach us to hate everything about ourselves and love and crave everything attached to them.

It's frustrating that this conversation falls on deaf ears, but there are moments of light. Moments that give humanity a little hope. Recent movement in the fight for Black lives in light of police brutality has been one of those hopeful moments. My only wish is that it can be sustained. That we can use what we learned from our ancestors, from our grandmothers and grandfathers, and leverage that wisdom to build a better world. Black and Brown folks are asking for equality. That's a reasonable request, especially considering the levels of inhumane treatment inflicted on our communities. But even more than that, we demand that the dominant culture own its documented history of injustices and work diligently to replace it with systems that intend good for *all*. The calls for reform and defunding the police are not without warrant. Danielle Sered, in *Until We Reckon*, speaks about the immediate need to address these injustices, and everything about my experience concurs. "It means not only shrinking systems but developing solutions that stand to displace them," she writes. "And it means building political power to protect those changes from backsliding and backlash. The people whose lives are at stake will need to have the durable collective power to choose, implement, and sustain solutions."

In short, the ruse is up. The curtains have been pulled back. We see the props on your stage, and we've got a copy of your script. We are no longer deceived by the lines you recite saying that the problems are "not that bad" or that we are the source of our own oppression. We're reading your script and can clearly see the stage notes that claim whiteness as the standard and everything else inferior. We see you. It's time you fix the problem and stop trying to apply Band-Aid reforms. They're not solutions; they're coverings. They don't allow for healing. They don't allow for our stories to breathe.

If my experience doesn't prove that America is sick, I don't know what does. If it can happen to me, it can happen to

At Harlem Valley.

anyone. My mission is to make sure it never happens again. To anyone. It's easy to feel trapped in a cycle of despair. It's easy to believe that you don't have tools to fight the good fight. But that's not true. Knowing yourself and identifying your power for yourself is the winning strategy for navigating the uneasiness of the rage we feel as Black or Brown people in America. It hurts to think that some people in our community took the forty-fifth president seriously during his 2016 campaign when he asked us, "What do you have to lose?"

A lot.

I know firsthand.

TWELVE

Becoming an Alchemist

And when you discover what you will be in your life, set out to do it as if God Almighty called you at this particular moment in history to do it.

REV. DR. MARTIN LUTHER KING JR.

THERE HAVE BEEN SO MANY times throughout the writing of this book when I've thought about the life I lived before the case. When I've really had to sit with the innocence and naivete that was stolen from me. There are small memories, things most people would laugh about at the family reunion or whisper about with close friends, that seem so much bigger, more notable, in the context of my life.

There's the time when David Nocenti, my Big Brother, bought me a skateboard. Skateboards were very expensive in the late '80s. The financial realities of most of the people in my neighborhood meant that parents weren't just running out buying top-of-the-line skateboards for their kids. If asked, a mama would likely say, "No. Make your own skateboard." And before David's gift, I'd done exactly that. Wheels were easy to find, so I added them to a little piece of metal piping along the bottom of a flat block of plywood to support my weight. As soon as my friends and I were riding down what we called "the Ramp" in Schomburg Plaza, we realized I could do some of the same tricks that kids on the expensive boards could do.

But the skateboard that David bought me was no DIY

project. It was an exclusive model, black and green, with a fin in the back. Anybody who was into skateboarding—and there was a crew of us in Harlem—wanted a board like mine with the rails underneath that allowed you to do tricks and slides. I did ollies, sharp turns; I was jumping off curbs and flipping the board. I was a real skateboarder, so this gift delighted me and meant so much.

Some days, I'd ride to school. If it was early enough, I'd enter Central Park at 110th Street and eventually end up on West Drive. That street had the best hills. Steep in parts, smooth in others. Sometimes I'd ride them. Other times I'd walk them. It didn't matter as long as I kept moving. I never thought about safety. Of course, I heard people talking about how dangerous the park was, especially in the '80s. But I knew Central Park as intimately as if it were my own backyard. In my youthfulness, I'd move through the park like Matthew Henson surveying the North Pole. In those moments I was an intrepid, fearless adventurer. Sure, I was an explorer on the way to school, but a fearless explorer nonetheless.

I savored the freedom that came with my skateboard. Riding alongside the cars, and in Central Park, I'd try to race them. Or make them stop for me. Call it a teenage power trip, but I thought it was cool that *I* could be the reason they would stop moving, and hit the brakes. On those morning rides to LaGuardia, I knew I was invincible. Until I wasn't.

It was around 103rd Street, on the west side of the park, when a group of Latino guys with sharpened screwdrivers confronted me.

"Yo, give us that board!"

They surrounded me. I was twelve or thirteen years old, and I was terrified. I took a beat to answer. But they didn't bother waiting for my response. They snatched the board out of my hands.

This was my first reality check. This was also the first time I remember being totally confused by cops; in my naivete, I believed that, for the most part, being around them meant I was safe. Almost immediately after the guys snatched the board, I turned around and saw two white officers standing right there. Both looked young. Maybe still in their twenties. One was heavier, like the stereotypical donut-eating cop. The other one was slim. I felt assured. I walked up to them. "Hey, these guys just stole my skateboard!"

Almost in slow motion—at least it felt that way—one of the cops turned to them and asked, "Hey, did you just steal his skateboard?"

The guys just started laughing. One said, "Man, we were just playing with him. That's all."

"Oh, okay. Good. Well, all right then."

And just like that, the cops walked away.

They're leaving?

My false sense of safety began to evaporate quickly. They didn't even bother to say, "Let me walk with you to get you out of this dangerous situation."

Of course they didn't.

When I turned back around, my new "friends" weren't too

happy. Their faces were grim. They proceeded to "run my pockets," patting me down to steal whatever else was on me. I have to admit, I was more hurt that they stole the cassette tapes in my pocket than I was to lose the board. Those tapes represented hours I'd spent customizing hip hop playlists for various occasions. Now they'd be enjoying the fruits of my labor.

When I told David what happened, he wasn't angry about it. In his laid-back way, he didn't even appear worried or upset. He also didn't say, "Oh, I'm so sorry" or offer any consolation. He just told me, "We're going to keep on moving forward. No worries."

I'm reminded of those moments of riding free in the park. Of dipping and swaying along concrete as trees bowed to me in the distance. I think about Central Park—the symbol of both my freedom and my bondage. How everything turned on me so very suddenly. One minute I was a kid racing cars on my skateboard, pretending to be a superhero in this vast greenery; the next minute my innocence and, soon after, my freedom were stolen. The first time was through neglect—two policemen leaving me to deal with danger on my own. The next time was due to a sinister plot to turn my Black body into another number in a prison jumpsuit.

∽

If I'm honest, writing this book has stretched me in ways I never imagined. It's forced emotions and memories to the surface that

I'd long put away. It was a challenge to sit in those feelings again in order to tell this story. I had to reckon with the impact of a trauma that, despite being thirty-plus years old, can still, in moments, feel fresh. There were many times over the course of these months when I had to relinquish my internal safety mechanism in order to get the words down. Creating distance, seeing *that* Yusef as different from the Yusef I've become, has helped me feel sane. But in order to be true to my experience, to my memories, I've had to reach back and grab fifteen-year-old Yusef's hand; I've had to hold his fears, sorrow, and pain, and let him know that everything will be okay—eventually.

I'll never forget one man whom I met in prison. He was Muslim as well, but he just approached life differently. He had an esoteric sensibility and would do things like read the Qur'an from the back to the front. He was also a martial artist.

Everyone called him Buddha. He was a big guy, his belly large and round. But he was also very quick on his feet. If he needed to take hold of somebody because things were about to get out of hand, that person had no hope of getting away.

One day he said to me, "Hey, I'm going to teach you something."

This was not long after I'd had my shoulder yanked out of its socket on the basketball court, and my arm was still in a sling.

"You need to learn tai chi."

I wasn't familiar with the form. At first, I thought it might be like jujitsu and other martial arts I was more familiar with, but this was very different. This was about healing.

"Everyone and everything has energy," he'd say. "Learn how to breathe, how to move your energy around."

When I figured out that tai chi could be used to not just heal myself in the moment—like my arm—but could help me move through bouts of emotional pain, I fell in love with it. I understood him when he'd say "Hold the ball" and would show me how there was energy moving against and away from it, that there was a way to harness that energy to push the ball where I needed it to go. That I could breathe from my center, from my belly button, to allow any negative energy to be moved out and to draw positivity in...It was mind-blowing!

But then Buddha took it a step further. He taught me Arnis, a Filipino fighting art that was supposed to be practiced with sticks. We were in prison, so sticks were not an option, but that didn't stop him from adapting the form to our circumstances. We did it without.

"I'm going to show you how to fight in an eight-pointed circle."

I can't lie. A part of me wondered why he was teaching me this. He didn't know me. I could have been the kind of person who would turn on him at any moment. But what I realized was that he'd been watching me. He was one of the people who must have thought, *This guy ain't supposed to be here and I need to help him. I need to give him the tools.*

"If—no, when—you get attacked in a yard and the whole yard is piling on, you must know how to fight more than just one person at a time."

He called over four of his buddies and said to us, "Okay, y'all, try to hit me." And we did.

His movements were swift and sharp. He'd turn one way and then another as if he sensed where the next blow might be coming from. He blocked hands and fists like the fighters I'd seen in the movies. Not a single one of us could touch him.

Before prison, I'd been taught by my martial arts instructors that anything could be a weapon. But I'd never actually seen it play out so precisely. Not a stick in sight.

"Eh, you get the *Source* magazine? If you roll that bad boy up, you can use the circle of it as a weapon," Buddha said. "You can use most anything to protect yourself."

It was true. And it was such an important lesson to learn when I was barely an adult and had been transferred to an adult correctional facility where I was imprisoned alongside people who had literally chopped up bodies. Martial arts was never about hurting anyone. It was about protecting; it was about healing.

An even more powerful weapon over the long term was my ability to meditate. This was also something I learned in prison.

As I continued to immerse myself in the Qur'an and synthesize what I was learning in its pages with what life had been teaching me so far, I began to understand that there were always higher principles at work. A wall is not solid. It's made up of millions of particles that are moving against each other. It's the laws we created that identify a wall as a solid structure. But what if we chose to live by other laws? Would that mean

I could see things—including my own circumstance, as awful and wrong as it was—differently? Was there a plane of existence I could access that would allow me to disconnect from the trauma? Through regular meditation, I learned that there was.

It was against the law to carry weapons in prison, but what if I made my fist into a weapon? Better yet, what if I could make my mind a weapon? Both would defend me. But the latter had the greater potential to free me. In my understanding of meditation, I realized that there were spiritual keys available to me. If I tapped in—used those keys to unlock my mind and spirit—then spiritual forces would come to my rescue; they would insulate me from the worst of my experience.

This sounds spookier than it actually is. You know that gut feeling you have as you walk along a dark street and contemplate taking a shortcut down an even darker alley? That feeling of apprehension is your guide. It's your body revealing to you what's happening in the spirit realm. You could still walk down that alley but maybe you pray as you do to activate the energy around you. Or maybe you simply go another direction.

There's a story I heard once, though I forget where, that perfectly illustrates this point of the true power we hold. There was a guy who saw a young woman walking down the street. He also saw a suspicious-looking man following her. He thought, *Hold on, let me follow them, just in case something happens. I want to be able to protect and help.* The man watches the guy follow the girl down a dark alley and just as he's about to turn down that same street in pursuit, the suspicious man runs back out of the alley, out of breath and looking like he'd just seen a ghost.

"Hey, what's up, man? Why are you running? What's going on?"

And the guy says, "Oh no! These two creatures just came out of nowhere and scared me. I don't know what that was!"

A few days later, the same man saw the woman. He stopped her and said, "Hey, the other day I saw you when you went down the alley. I was a little concerned because it was dark and late. There was a guy following you. Why'd you go that way? What happened? What were you doing when you went down the alley?"

She said, "I wasn't doing anything special. I was just listening to the Qur'an."

I've learned to pay attention to what my life is teaching me, and what I know for sure is that it's imperative we become our own personal activists. It's critical that we stand up to injustice, but while we are doing that collectively, we must also be willing to transform any personal experiences of negativity into positive ones to help drive our success.

An alchemist is formally defined as a person who transforms or creates something through a seemingly magical process. That's who I've attempted to become in the time since I was released. It hasn't been easy, and I've made a million mistakes along the way, but I've always kept in mind the significance of combating this negative narrative, and I'm always looking for tangible ways to keep my peace.

No matter your faith tradition, or if you don't have a religious affiliation at all, there's something nearly supernatural that happens when you decide to take control over your mind. No matter how hard and devastating our circumstances might be, there is a higher consciousness working on our behalf. In the same way we don't see the air we breathe but trust that it's filling our lungs and keeping us alive, there is something that can keep you going if you are willing to tap into it long enough to allow that good energy to fill you.

Plugging into a higher spirituality allows you to say, "Oh wow, there's my reality, but there's also a greater truth I can strive for." Through meditation and learning about mindfulness, I realized that I was truly an active participant in my life. And meditation didn't have to look like me sitting cross-legged in my room, chanting. I could meditate while I walked. I could control my breathing, no matter where I happened to be. Whether I was inside the prison walls or sitting in my backyard thirty years later, I could control both my physical and my spiritual outlooks. I could move the negative energy that tells my body to be depressed or my mind to rage and channel it into something positive.

That's the reason why I loved Paulo Coelho's novel *The Alchemist* when I first read it a few years ago. The allegorical story of a young boy searching for his personal legend, being met with obstacles along his journey, resonated with me so much. One of the central takeaways repeated throughout the book is: *When you want something, the entire universe conspires in helping you to achieve it.*

In a way, I think that's what I've been getting at in writing this book. It's important to me that you know my story. But ultimately what I want to say is, if you remain a person of great character and integrity and continue to grow and develop yourself, then no one can truly define you. God, the universe, whatever you believe in, will conspire to get you to your purpose. That doesn't mean you won't go through the fire to get there. I sure did. But what you learn along the way will become powerful tools that you will wield faithfully in the end. We must become our own personal alchemists and embrace the transformation that will come as we move through this life.

So here we are, back at acceptance. Wherever you are—a jail cell, a cubicle, a pew—I would recommend leaning into some deep reflection. Sometimes we resist the memories. We don't want to go back there or relive a moment. And you know I get that. Reflection can be painful. But without it, you can't get to the transformation. Like the symbol of Sankofa in West African spirituality, you have to be able to look backward even as you are moving forward. To see how far you've come. To know which way to go.

Yes, you might be walking through hell, but you can also walk right through it and come out on the other side just like the three Hebrew boys Shadrach, Meshach, and Abednego—*without even the smell of smoke on you.* Here's the catch, though: Coming out of your hell might mean walking a path that hasn't been charted yet. One that your mother or grandmother, your uncles and brothers, cannot even fathom. Like me, you may have to create your path from the scorched earth of a life this world tried to steal from you. That's okay. Just grab your proverbial machete and chop down the weeds trying to cover your way. You do it not only for yourself. By virtue of your courage and persistence, you will make a path for all those behind you who are also seeking a way out.

Whatever you do, as you are reflecting on your past, do not become bitter. Dr. Maya Angelou's words resonate with me. She said, "You should be angry. But you must not be bitter. Bitterness is like cancer. It eats upon the host. It doesn't do anything to the object of its displeasure. So use that anger. You write it. You paint it. You dance it. You march it. You vote it. You do everything about it. You talk it. Never stop talking it."

Angelou was teaching us how to become alchemists. How to use the circumstances of our lives to our benefit. How to allow God to work out our pain for our good. How to speak of our story so that others will know they aren't alone on this journey. When I tell my story, as I have in this book, I'm taking back my power from those who tried to cage me. If I simply let others tell my story, then I will lose it. But once I speak for myself, I turn pain into prosperity and triumph. Only I have the power to shape my narrative. I take the tragedy of the Central Park jogger case and turn it into an opportunity to make sure no other young person becomes one of the Central Park Five. *That* is alchemy.

To transform your experience, you must take the emotions that come up in your reflection and move that energy into something purposeful. In reflecting on the trauma you've experienced in order to figure out how to heal going forward, anger may show up. And it's okay. Anger is a valid and necessary response. The question is, what will you do with that anger? Will you turn it outward toward others or upon your own child? Or will you dance with it a bit? Defuse it with love for yourself. Leaning into these feelings, not running away, is what helps release them. Ignoring and pushing those feelings down only allows them to take root as bitterness. The lemons stay lemons and never become the sweetness of lemonade. But giving your story air, not holding your breath, is what gives you back the power.

I know that there are those who don't have the resources or opportunity to even be able to consider diving into their past. Their lives are consumed by getting through the next minute or hour. Maybe they've just been released from jail, and their friend from the streets just picked them up.

Welcome home! I got the ladies lined up for you. I got the drugs you like. I got the drinks you like.

But this guy is trying to start his life over again. He wants to become an alchemist but doesn't know where to begin. I know that feeling, too. Here's where it gets incredibly simple, although admittedly it's not easy. The first step is always found in the first choice.

In that moment, because of his first choice, the universe shifts on this man's behalf. God begins to orchestrate all that is to come for his good. Like Coelho's character Santiago, a singular choice sets in motion other opportunities that might not have existed had he not made it. It's always about making the next right choice.

I could have decided that because the system had railroaded me, stolen years of my life, I would simply give up on trying to live up to the title of Master that my grandmother gave me. But choice often indicates what happens next. To choose life in the midst of opposition gives you a chance at living. Choosing death in the midst of that same opposition only ensures death. Both are painful. Both require the kinds of shifts in mind-set that are often hard in today's society. But I believe that there comes a time when the pain of remaining the same is far greater than the pain of trying to do something different, and that's when transformation actually happens.

The one thing we have power over is how much learning we decide to take on. Malcolm X told us that being educated gives us more options than one. If we need help making a choice, then that help can often be found in a book. And even when the books are taken away, there is always a way to get the answer. Black folks, in particular, come from this kind of resilience.

The system is running exactly the way it was designed to. It profits from Black and Brown bodies and keeps many of us locked into a perpetual state of fear and exhaustion in trying to prove our humanity. And yet, you have control only over yourself. You have control over how you process your memories. Over whether or not you believe in yourself enough to pour grace on your flaws and allow love to quell bitterness. I was put away as a fifteen-year-old child and came home a twenty-three-year-old child. For a time, I had to deal with myself as I figured out what being an adult looked like for me. As the alchemist of your life, you have control over the choices you make on this journey. One choice at a time. And it might take time.

But no matter what, you *can* be free.

Acknowledgments

I'd like to think of *Better, Not Bitter* as more than just a story—it's a love offering.

It is an offering of love and empathy to the millions who have gone through the criminal system of injustice, those who were pushed to the margins of society and/or who had their voices turned down. An offering that reaffirms my dedication to restoring their humanity.

This offering wouldn't be possible without the support of countless individuals who have helped me in my journey, guided me in my darkest hours, and inspired me to water the seeds of greatness that exist in every member of the kaleidoscope of the human family.

To my umi, Sharonne Salaam, who raised me to recognize my true value in a society where the worth of Black life has always been "less than," a *proportion of potential.*

You have always been my guide and the embodiment of the conscience of Black humanity. You've told me when to love, when to have faith, but most important, when to refuse to participate in the system—just as you told me in that interrogation room so many years ago.

I have no words to describe my love for you, and I am thankful to you and to Allah for placing you in my life.

A special offering of love to my wife, Sanovia, and our blended family (in order): Nahtique, Dimani, Rain, Winter, Aaliyah, Poetry, Onaya, Ameerah, Assata, and baby Yusef Amir Idris. Thank you for your patience, your grace, and your support during this process.

Thank you to my sister, Aisha, and to my brother, Shareef, for showing me how dedication, planning, and desire can turn a dream into reality.

To the eternal sacred brotherhood now known as the Exonerated Five—Korey, Raymond, Antron, and Kevin—together we suffered through a collective silence and a collective despair that only we truly understand, yet the bond we forged can never be broken.

I wish nothing but blessings upon each of my brothers as we embark on our own unique journeys. I know silence was forced upon us, but our voices will inspire change.

Thank you to Ken Burns, Sarah Burns, and Dave McMahon for shining a spotlight on us through the *Central Park Five* documentary and bringing us out of the darkness.

To Ava DuVernay—the vision and honesty of *When They See Us* showcased our story to the world, and the world listened. The power of your art has elevated us to new heights, and I cannot be more grateful.

To my team, Frank Harris and Travis Linton at 23 Management; to my team at CAA; and to my PR team at Sunshine

Sachs—thank you for being honest, willing, and capable partners. I am proud to have you in my corner every step of the way.

To Seema Mahanian, Linda Duggins, Brian McLendon, Carolyn Kurek, and Albert Tang at Grand Central Publishing, for giving me the opportunity to tell my story and believing in my potential to inspire.

To the late Maya Angelou, whose work inspired the title of my memoir and continues to guide me throughout my life.

And finally, none of this would have been possible without the incredible support of a brilliant collaborative mind, Tracey Lewis-Giggetts. As I embarked on this journey of telling my story, Tracey was my pilot, my conductor, my shepherd. I am so proud of the bond of trust we have built throughout the creation of *Better, Not Bitter*, and I am so proud that I can now call you my friend in life.

I often say that for us to truly move forward, we—the collective we—must have a Sankofa moment, where we reach back and gather the best of what our past has to teach us so that we can achieve our full potential.

I thank the ancestors for instilling that generational potential within all of us—from the first stolen Black body that landed on American shores, to the men and women who were brutally beaten for protecting their right to vote, to five boys convicted of a crime they did not commit.

I offer *Better, Not Bitter* to spark our moment of truth: that *we* are our ancestors' wildest dreams, and we can achieve anything we want to do.

All we have to do is get started.

Suggested Reading List

Aberjhani. *Illuminated Corners: Collected Essays and Articles.* Vol. 1. Unpublished.

Alexander, Michelle. *The New Jim Crow: Mass Incarceration in the Age of Colorblindness.* Rev. ed. New York: New Press, 2012.

Ani, Marimba. *Yurugu: An African-Centered Critique of European Cultural Thought and Behavior.* Trenton, NJ: Africa World Press, 1994.

Bawa Muhaiyaddeen, M. R. *Asma'ul Husna: The 99 Beautiful Names of Allah.* Philadelphia: Fellowship Press, 1979.

Bradley, Michael, and John Henrik Clarke. *The Iceman Inheritance: Prehistoric Sources of Western Man's Racism, Sexism and Aggression.* Toronto: Dorset, 1978.

Coelho, Paulo. *The Alchemist.* New York: HarperSanFrancisco, 1994.

Cress Welsing, Frances. *The Isis Papers: The Keys to the Colors.* Chicago: Third World Press, 1991.

Du Bois, W. E. B. *The Souls of Black Folk.* Edited by Brent Hayes Edwards. Oxford: Oxford University Press, 2008.

Haley, Alex. *Roots: The Saga of an American Family.* New York: Doubleday, 1976.

Kendi, Ibram X. *How to Be an Antiracist.* New York: One World, 2019.

Kenyatta, Jomo. *Facing Mount Kenya: The Tribal Life of the Gikuyu.* New York: Vintage Books, 1965.

Kerik, Bernard B. *From Jailer to Jailed: My Journey from Correction and Police Commissioner to Inmate #84888-054.* New York: Simon & Schuster, 2015.

Khan-Cullors, Patrisse, and Asha Bandele. *When They Call You a Terrorist: A Black Lives Matter Memoir.* New York: St. Martin's Press, 2018.

Kloss, Jethro. *Back to Eden: The Classic Guide to Herbal Medicine, Natural Foods, and Home Remedies Since 1939.* Detroit: Lotus Press, 2004.

Sered, Danielle. *Until We Reckon: Violence, Mass Incarceration, and a Road to Repair.* New York: New Press, 2019.

Sogoba, Mia. "The Power of a Name." February 11, 2019. Cultures of West Africa. https://www.culturesofwestafrica.com/power-of-names/.

Van der Kolk, Bessel. *The Body Keeps the Score: Brain, Mind, and Body in the Healing of Trauma.* New York: Viking, 2014.

West, Cornel, and Christa Buschendorf. *Black Prophetic Fire.* Boston: Beacon Press, 2014.

About the Author

YUSEF SALAAM is the inspirational speaker and prison abo-
litionist who at age fifteen was one of the five teenage boys
wrongly convicted and sentenced to prison in the Central Park
jogger case. In 1997, he left prison as an adult to a world he
didn't fully recognize or understand. In 2002, the sentences for
the Central Park Five were overturned, and all five were exonerated for the crime they didn't commit. Yusef now travels the
world as an inspirational speaker, talking about the effects of
incarceration and the devastating impact of disenfranchisement.
He is an advocate and educator on issues of mass incarceration,
police brutality and misconduct, press ethics and bias, race and
law, and the disparities in the criminal justice system, especially
for men of color.